MICHAEL ASKS WHY

ELLEN G. WHITE'S
CLASSIC
*THE GREAT
CONTROVERSY*
ADAPTED FOR
CHILDREN

SALLY PIERSON DILLON

Pacific Press® Publishing Association
Nampa, Idaho
Oshawa, Ontario, Canada

Edited by B. Russell Holt
Designed by Dennis Ferree
Inside art by Phyllis Cahill
Cover art by Carol Strebel

Unless otherwise indicated, all Bible verses are quoted from the *International Children's Bible, New Century Version,* copyright © 1986 by Worthy Publishing, Forth Worth, Texas 76137. Used by permission.

Library of Congress Cataloging-in-Publication Data

Dillon, Sally Pierson, 1959-
    Michael asks why : Ellen G. White's classic The Great Controversy adapted for children/Sally Pierson Dillon.
        p. cm.
        Summary: A Seventh-day Adventist mother explains to her son the history and development of the Christian church from the first century to today, emphasizing the Protestant Reformation, the history of religion in America, and various Biblical prophecies.
    ISBN 0-8163-1759-3 (paper)
    1. Seventh-day Adventists—Doctrines—Juvenile literature. [1. Seventh-day Adventists—Doctrines. 2. Christianity.] I. White, Ellen Gould Harmon, 1827-1915. The great controversy and Bible made plain. II. Title.

BX6121 D55 2000
286.7'32—dc21   99-049058

00 01 02 03 04 • 5 4 3 2

CONTENTS

Dedication:
To Michael Dillon, the thinker, for asking so many questions; and to Don and Betty Pierson, my parents, for telling me these stories and teaching me what I needed to know to answer Michael's questions.

Acknowledgements:
This book would not be in your hands today were it not for the help of many dedicated people. Thank you to all of them. Virginia Smith, Director of the General Conference Children's Ministries Department, was the catalyst in making this project actually happen. Elder Robert J. Kloosterhuis forged the way for it to be published. Ruth Satelmajer brought the E. G. White Estate on board. Denice Grove and LuWana Kumalae spent countless hours typing the manuscript. The Pacific Press® Publishing Association produced the big mylar edition of *The Triumph of God's Love* with the beautiful color pictures that captured Michael's attention and made him ask, "Why?"

INTRODUCTION
FOR PARENTS

The conversations in this book actually took place between Michael and me. We had recently read *Margie Asks Why,* and Michael still had questions. We sat together, leafing through a large copy of *The Great Controversy,* by Ellen G. White, looking at the color illustrations as I answered his questions and described the stories portrayed in the pictures.

Margie Asks Why is a wonderful book for explaining the origin of sin and suffering and the plan of salvation to primary-age children. But it stops at the ascension of Jesus. What happened after that? Why do we believe what we do? And what is going to happen next? *The Great Controversy* addresses each of these issues. The first third of the book tells the story of the Protestant Reformation. The book then goes on to reveal the evolution of our specific Seventh-day Adventist beliefs, followed by Ellen G. White's step-by-step description of the end time and Jesus' second coming. All this—along with the Adventist understanding of the sanctuary, the atonement, the millennium, our homecoming to the new earth, and the final judgment—is explained to Michael's satisfaction.

This book is not for children who know nothing of God and His plan of salvation. To be of benefit, the readers (and listeners) need to have already heard the basic Bible stories. Only then can they fit all those things into their own frame of reference. *Michael Asks Why* should not be considered a substitute for *Margie Asks Why* but perhaps a sequel. The purpose of this book is (a) to provide information for your children and answers to their questions, (b) to firmly ground them in their beliefs and the biblical basis for them, and (c) to help prepare them for Jesus' soon coming and the investigative judgment—and to anticipate both with joy and confidence.

This book has forty-two chapters, each covering the same material as the corresponding chapter in *The Great Controversy*. The vocabulary, chapter length, and complexity is adapted for the eight- to ten-year-old child. These conversations took place when Michael was seven years old. Michael had a strong religious background and was therefore ready to understand this information.

The average eight year old will not find this book easy to read alone. It was designed for adult/child interaction, such as Michael and I shared. I strongly suggest that you read this *with* your child. Discuss points of interest and do the activities in the accompanying activity book together. The interaction between Michael and me offers a model for parent-child interaction and spiritual nurture. Obviously, it was not possible to include all the details from the more than six hundred pages in *The Great Controversy*. But all of the important concepts are here. I strongly encourage parents to read the corresponding chapters in *The Great Controversy* for more information and to answer questions your child may ask that Michael didn't.

It is my greatest hope that the purposes of this book will be met—that you and your child will both become more firmly grounded in Jesus and more confident daily in His ability to see you safely through to your home in the new earth.

Sally Pierson Dillon

INTRODUCTION

Michael wandered into the kitchen where Mother was chopping carrots. She smiled as he parked himself on a stool next to her. "I've been thinking," he began.

"Oh no!" said Mother, "Does it hurt?"

Michael laughed. "No! I've been thinking about your friend, Mrs. Dean. I heard her say that her church was the only real Christian church and that all the other churches broke off from her church. She said her church is still the same as when Jesus' disciples started it in the first place. Is that true?"

"Well," said Mother, "my friend Nicki Dean belongs to the Russian Orthodox Church."

"What is that?" asked Michael.

"Right after Jesus went back to heaven," said Mother, "there was only one Christian church. For about a thousand years there was one official church. Then the leaders had a big disagreement, and the church split into two groups. Each claimed to be the true church. The Eastern group called itself the Orthodox Church. Their church is still around; it's known as the *Greek* Orthodox, or the *Russian* Orthodox, or the *Eastern* Orthodox Church, depending on the language used. The other church group stayed in the western part of Europe, and for a long time they were the official Christian church there. Today, that church is known as the Roman Catholic Church."

"Oh," said Michael. "So the Orthodox feel that the Roman Catholics split off of their group?"

"Yes," said Mother.

"Well, why are there so many churches today? There are hardly any Catholics in our neighborhood, and Mrs. Dean is the only Orthodox person I know. But there are lots of Baptists and Methodists and Lutherans and Episcopalians and even a few Seventh-day Adventists. Where did they all come from?"

"Whoa!" said Mother. "One question at a time!"

"And," said Michael, "how come, even though Christians are supposed to be kind and to love each other, they do so many mean things? I know they did mean things a long time ago in history, like persecuting people and killing them and stuff like that, but Christians are still doing mean things. On the news, there was a Christian guy in Florida who was threatening some people at a clinic, and someone else shot a doctor and other people who worked there. And the news was also talking about Christians bombing each other in Ireland. Christians shouldn't be bombing anyone, should they, Mom?"

"No," answered Mother, "not if they are living the way Jesus taught them to."

"There's some other stuff that I was wondering too," said Michael. Mother swallowed her further explanation and sat down to listen.

"Our church believes a lot of the same stuff as other churches. The people I know who aren't Adventists just seem to believe one or two things differently than we do. But the different things depend on what church they're from."

Introduction

"Yes, that's true," said Mother.

"I know the things I believe that are different," said Michael, "but I'm not always sure why I believe them. Especially the *really* different things, like whether dead people are really dead and how come we worship on Sabbath instead of Sunday. And what is this 'sanctuary' I hear you talk about sometimes? Why is it important?"

"That's an easy one," said Mother. "I can answer that for you." But Michael was on a roll.

"Something else . . . at school we were talking about Jesus coming again and how soon it's going to be, especially with all the stuff going on in the news. Some kids were really scared and were talking about terrible things that were going to happen. I wasn't scared until they started talking about it, but now I'm really worried. How can I be ready for Jesus to come again? And how do I know that I am ready? And how can I face the terrible things that will happen without being afraid? I feel really worried about it right now!"

Mother put her arm around Michael. "You've asked about fifty important questions in the last ten minutes," she said. "What if we take some time every day, right after you finish your homework, and talk about them? We'll start with what happened after Jesus went back to heaven and bring you right up to today. And then we'll talk about the future."

"That sounds great," said Michael. "So how about *before* I do my homework?"

"Nice try." Mother laughed.

"I guess I'll go start on my homework, then," Michael sighed.

1
Jesus Loves Everyone

"Mom, I'm ready," Michael called. "My homework is all done."

"Good," said Mother. She sat down on the bed next to Michael. "Do you remember what happened right before Jesus was crucified in Jerusalem?"

"I think so," said Michael. "What do you want to know about?"

"Jesus' triumphal entry."

"Sure," said Michael. "Jesus came riding into Jerusalem on a donkey, and all the people shouted 'Hosanna' and were really excited. When Jesus got to the top of the hill and looked down into Jerusalem, He started to cry."

"Do you know why?" asked Mother.

"Because He knew Jerusalem would be destroyed someday."

"Yes," said Mother. "The destruction of Jerusalem and its people was awful. Jesus was able to look into the future and see what was going to happen, and it broke His heart. Jesus warned His disciples and followers. He told them exactly what would happen and when they should escape. You can find what He said in Matthew 23 and 24."

MICHAEL ASKS WHY

"OK," said Michael. He read Matthew 23:37–24:3 from his Bible.

Jerusalem, Jerusalem! You kill the prophets and kill with stones those men God sent to you. Many times I wanted to help your people! I wanted to gather them together as a hen gathers her chicks under her wings. But you did not let me. Now your home will be left completely empty. I tell you, you will not see me again until that time when you will say, "God bless the One who comes in the name of the Lord." Jesus left the Temple and was walking away. But his followers came to show him the Temple's buildings. Jesus asked, "Do you see all these buildings? I tell you the truth. Every stone will be thrown down to the ground. Not one stone will be left on another."

Michael looked at Mother. Then he read Jesus' explanation of what would happen during this time (verses 9-12):

"Then men will arrest you and hand you over to be hurt and kill you. They will hate you because you believe in me. At that time, many who believe will lose their faith. They will turn against each other and hate each other. Many false prophets will come and cause many people to believe false things. There will be more and more evil in the world. So most people will stop showing their love for each other."

"Now read Luke 21:20, 21," Mother said.
Michael read:

"When you see armies all around Jerusalem, then you will know that it will soon be destroyed. At that time, the people in Judea should run away to the mountains. The people in Jerusalem must get out. If you are near the city, don't go in!"

12

Jesus Loves Everyone

"Good," said Mom. "So Jesus told them that when they saw soldiers surrounding Jerusalem, they should escape. For forty years, after Jesus gave all of these warnings, everything went on day after day, just the same. But Jesus' followers remembered His warnings and watched and waited. People became more and more wicked. The love of many did grow cold toward each other. Even in families, they betrayed and killed each other. All of Jesus' predictions came true.

"Many other strange things happened that made people afraid. In the middle of the night, a bright light shone on the altar in the temple. The earth trembled. The great eastern gate was so large it took twenty men to close it. It was kept shut with great bars of iron fastened deep into the street that was paved with solid stone. Yet it opened by itself at midnight. People started wondering, 'Is it time to go? Should we run away?' The priests paid false prophets to say the people should stay and wait, that everything was fine. Everything was happening just as Jesus had said.

"The Roman soldiers surrounded Jerusalem and wouldn't let anyone go in or out. Was this the sign Jesus had talked about? Not quite yet, because no one could get food or water or escape. They were slowly being starved into surrender.

"But just when the people in Jerusalem were about to give up, the Roman general and his armies suddenly left! The soldiers in Jerusalem ran after them, attacking those in the rear. They poured out of the city and grabbed any belongings the Romans had left behind. Now there was no one—neither the people of Jerusalem nor Romans—to stop God's people from fleeing from the city. The Christians recognized this as their sign to escape, and they did. They fled to the town of Pella in the mountains across the Jordan River. But the people who didn't believe Jesus' warnings went back into the city to celebrate, carrying all the things they had stolen from the Roman camp.

"However, General Titus soon returned with a huge Roman army. Again, he surrounded the city, and thousands of people died from hunger and disease. Whenever the Romans captured someone, they treated their prisoners cruelly and then crucified them just outside the city wall. Mrs. White tells about this in a book called *The Great Controversy.* God showed her things that had happened long ago as well as things in the future and told her to write them down so people could understand what they all meant. Mrs. White said that there were so many crosses around Jerusalem and nearby that there was hardly enough room to move between them.

"When Titus attacked Jerusalem, Roman soldiers poured into the city, killing people as they went. Titus told his soldiers not to touch the temple. However, a soldier threw a flaming torch into the temple, and soon smoke was billowing out of it. The soldiers swarmed in and killed the people who had gathered there thinking they would be safe."

"Wow!" said Michael. "And Jesus was seeing all of this in the future when He was on the donkey up on the hill?"

"Yes," said Mother.

"No wonder He cried!" said Michael.

"It made Jesus very sad," Mother said. "More than a million people were killed. Even though they had rejected Him, Jesus loved them so much. But we need to remember that when Jerusalem was destroyed, not one person died who listened to Jesus' warnings and did what He told them to do. Jesus had told them ahead of time what was going to happen, and He took care of them during the siege of Jerusalem."

"Wow!" said Michael. "You mean not one Christian died?"

"Not one," said Mother. "Look in your Bible again and read what Jesus said."

Michael took several minutes and read the whole chapter of Matthew 24. Then he said, "Is Jesus talking here just about the destruction of Jerusalem? It sounds like He's talking about the end of the world and the Second Coming too."

"That's right," said Mother. "He was describing both things. And, if Jesus could take care of all the Christians back then when Jerusalem was destroyed, don't you think He can take care of us during the difficult days when He comes again? Do you think we need to be afraid of the things that will happen just before the Second Coming?"

"No," said Michael, "I don't think so. I feel better about that now."

2

Faithful Christians

"Hey Mom!" said Michael as he burst into the kitchen.

"Hi, Michael. You're back from your trip."

"It was really great," said Michael. "We went to this old church in Washington, D.C. called the Franciscan Monastery. And underneath they had built almost an exact copy of something called the 'catacombs' from Rome."

"Really?" said Mother.

"Yeah," said Michael, "it was lots of tunnels under the ground, with little rooms where Christians used to hide—not in Washington, of course, but in Rome. They had to hide because they were being persecuted. They lived down there, had their church services down there, and even buried dead people down there. Of course, there weren't any real dead people down there where we were today in Washington because these catacombs were built just to look at. But the ones in Rome had real people in them."

"Yes, I know," said Mother. "I visited the real catacombs in Rome when I was a little girl."

MICHAEL ASKS WHY

"Wow!" said Michael. "I think they're neat. That would be so much fun to live underground."

Mother smiled. "Actually, I think it must have been kind of hard for the early Christians. First of all, they were living underground because they were treated so unkindly that they were afraid to come out. Also, the catacombs you saw today were built for people to take tours through. They are kept nice and clean. The ones in Rome were cold and damp, with lots of muddy places in them, and they smelled musty and moldy. They didn't have electricity for lights or fans or air conditioning or even heat. So it was probably dark and stuffy."

"Well, they could have taken big torches in there," said Michael.

"Yes," said Mother, "and then it would have been smokey."

"Oh," said Michael. "I guess it wasn't the greatest place to live, but at least they were safe down there."

"That's right," said Mom. "They were hiding because life was hard for Christians during those times. Some of them were thrown to wild animals and killed, and others were burned. Still others were crucified, and some were even covered with bloody animal skins and fed to wild dogs."

"That's horrible!" said Michael.

"Yes," said Mother, "but what made it even more horrible was that many people in Rome actually enjoyed watching the Christians suffer and be killed; they considered it entertainment! Christians had to choose whether to give up their religion or face one of these horrible deaths. Some Christians remained strong and faithful to what they believed. Others looked for an easier way to live.

"Most of the people in Rome were not Christians; they worshiped the emperor and all kinds of gods. They were called 'pagans.' Some Christians found if they mixed their Christian beliefs with the beliefs of their pagan Roman neighbors, they didn't have to worry as much about being persecuted. So they took idols that the pagans had worshiped for years and put them in their Christian churches and called them by the names of Bible characters—Joseph or the Virgin Mary or the apostles. So Christian beliefs and pagan beliefs got all mixed up together."

"Is that where statues of the saints started?" asked Michael.

"Yes," said Mother. "Now there was a split within the church. One group wanted to be more like the pagans and bring some of its ideas and practices into the Christian church. Another wanted to keep its worship and religion simple, as Jesus had taught, and base it only on the Scriptures. The group who tried to be more like its pagan Roman neighbors was not persecuted, and it felt that giving up some of its beliefs was worth it.

"Why is there not much persecution going on today?" Michael wanted to know. "I don't know anyone who is being forced to give up his faith in Jesus."

"Some people believe," said Mother, "that the reason is because most Christians have not been faithful to the simple ways that Jesus taught us to worship Him. Like some of the early Christians in Rome, Christians today have become so much like their non-Christian neighbors that the church has become popular, and there isn't much persecution.

"But in some places in the world, there *is* persecution going on today. In these places, Christians today have to decide to be true to Christ no matter what. As a result, the church is strong and growing in these places. Mrs. White tells us that if there was a true revival of faith among Christians everywhere, persecution would start again."

"Hmm," said Michael, thinking hard.

"Who do you think would pick on Christians the most," asked Mother, "the people who don't believe in Jesus at all or unfaithful Christians who have become like the pagans and are mad at those who won't be like them?"

"Probably the unfaithful Christians," said Michael.

"You're exactly right," said Mother.

3

Rejecting
God's Word

"What were some of the other changes Christians made besides using idols and not following the Bible exactly?" asked Michael.

"Well, Sunday keeping was one," said Mother.

"But Jesus didn't go to church on Sunday, did He?" asked Michael.

"No," said Mother. "Jesus was a Jew; the Bible tells us it was His habit to go to the synagogue every Sabbath. For the first two hundred years after Jesus went back to heaven, Christians still worshiped on Sabbath. The pagans who lived around them worshiped the sun on Sunday. This was a day of great celebration. Sabbath keeping, in contrast, was not nearly so boisterous. The Sunday celebrations looked like a lot more fun to some Christians. They started calling their day of worship 'the old Jewish Sabbath.' Little by little, they started celebrating Sunday, saying that they were honoring Jesus' resurrection. Of course, there is no evidence in the Bible that Jesus had ever asked anyone to worship Him on

Rejecting God's Word

Sunday. But Bibles were scarce, and most Christians didn't have one. So before long, very few Christians continued keeping the seventh-day Sabbath."

"What were some of the other changes?" asked Michael.

"Well," said Mother, "when Jesus went back to heaven, He went back to be our High Priest in the sanctuary in heaven. That means that He is our Mediator."

"What's a mediator?" asked Michael.

"A mediator is a person who tries to reconcile two people or two sides. For example, if two of your friends are having a disagreement, you might talk with both of them and help them to be friends again. That's a mediator," Mom explained. "Jesus is a Mediator because He works to bring us back into friendship with His Father.

"About this time, the leader of the official Christian church decided that if anyone wanted to talk to God or ask for forgiveness, he or she should go to the church and tell a church leader. Then the leader would talk directly to God for that person. No one could talk to God except through him. Imagine having to go to a church leader every time you wanted to talk to God! When the church leader decided he should talk to God for everyone, he was taking Jesus' job. Jesus said, 'No one comes to the Father but by Me.' "

"Don't some Christians today feel that the Virgin Mary is like that?" asked Michael. "That she talks to Jesus for us?"

"Yes," answered Mother.

"That isn't right," said Michael, "that is ignoring Jesus."

"True," said Mother, "that *is* ignoring Jesus. Remember why Jesus died on the cross?"

"Yes, He died to do away with our sins."

"And was Jesus' life and death on the cross enough to do away with all of our sins?" asked Mother.

"Sure," said Michael.

"Well," Mother continued, "as time went on, Satan caused the early Christians to add more and more requirements to what Jesus had already done on the cross. Christians believed they had to earn forgiveness by things they did—by making special trips to holy places or doing penance, which could be anything from saying several prayers to whipping themselves or paying money. Instead of relying on Jesus to save them, they tried to earn salvation themselves."

Michael wrinkled his forehead as he thought hard. "But, Mom, none of those things could do away with their sins. The only thing that can do away with sin is Jesus' death on the cross."

"You're right," agreed Mother, "but for hundreds of years, Satan deceived people into thinking that they had to do all of these other things, too, if they were going to be forgiven. Many of them were sincere people who loved God and wanted to do what was right. They had just been taught wrong, and there were no Bibles for them to read and learn the truth. So they worked hard to earn their way to heaven. They worshiped idols, burned candles, prayed to images, and paid the priests to plead with God for them."

"That's so sad," said Michael. "The Christian church claimed to worship Jesus, but it was ignoring Him and all the things He did on earth and the things He was doing in heaven. That must have really hurt His feelings."

"Yes," said Mother, "probably so. Then the leader of the official church (who was called the 'pope') made another announcement. He said that the church had never made any mistakes nor would it ever make any mistakes in the future, according to the Scriptures. Of course, the Scriptures didn't say this, but hardly anyone had a Bible, so almost no one could look it up.

"When King Henry IV came to the pope's castle to talk to him in the middle of winter, the pope wouldn't let him in all the way. He made the king wait in an outer court. Standing there in the snow in his bare feet, with no warm clothes on, King Henry waited to talk to the pope. For three days he waited before the pope let him come inside to talk to him."

"Three days!" Michael exclaimed. Jesus never treated people mean like that!"

Rejecting God's Word

"That's right," said Mother. "And we should all try to be like Jesus, whether we are church leaders, moms, or school kids."

"Were there other changes in the church?" asked Michael.

"Oh yes," said Mother. "The first Christians believed that when a person died, he stayed dead until the day God will wake him up again in the resurrection."

"Right," said Michael, "that's what we believe too."

"Yes, but since Christians had now come to pray to statues of saints and the disciples, they no longer believed that these people were really dead. They believed that the saints and the good people who had died must be in heaven. If so, then the bad people must not be dead either. They were probably in hell, a place where they burned for ever and ever and ever."

"Oh!" said Michael, "I think the bad people would be better off just dead, like we believe."

Mom smiled. "These Christians also believed in another place called 'purgatory,' a place halfway between heaven and hell."

"Who went there?" asked Michael. "The people who were only sort of good, or not quite good enough for heaven?"

"Yes," said Mom. "The church leaders then asked their relatives to say special prayers and buy special candles to burn for their loved ones who might be in purgatory. People paid lots of money so the people they loved could go from purgatory to heaven."

"But," said Michael, "if the people they loved who had died were really just dead in the ground, waiting for Jesus to wake them up again, then the church leaders were just taking all their money for nothing."

"That's right," Mother agreed. "And there was another change that took place. Remember the Last Supper that Jesus had with His disciples right before His crucifixion?"

"Yes," said Michael. "That's where our Communion service comes from."

"And what do we do in Communion?" asked Mother.

"We drink grape juice to remind us of Jesus' blood, and we eat little pieces of cracker bread to remind us of His body that He gave for us."

Mom nodded. "Those are symbols that remind us of Jesus and what He did for us because He loves us so much. Satan caused the Christians to believe that when they drank the grape juice it actually turned into Jesus' real blood and that when they ate the bread, they were actually eating Jesus' real body! They believed the bread and the grape juice weren't just symbols anymore but real flesh and blood."

"Oh," said Michael, "that's gross! They couldn't really be eating flesh and drinking blood, could they?"

"No," said Mother. "It was still just bread and grape juice. But they believed it was the real body and blood of Jesus. That's the difference between Communion and Mass.

"All of these changes and compromises came into the church and were taught to the people. Many of the people who were in the Christian church at that time were good people who loved God."

"I guess if they had no Bibles," said Michael, "they couldn't really help believing what they were taught."

"No, they couldn't. But God had a plan for sharing the truth with people so they wouldn't have to stay confused."

"God's always really good about that," said Michael.

Mother smiled. "Yes, He is, and we'll talk about it tomorrow evening."

4

The Bible in the Mountains

Michael closed his books and put away his pencils and paper. "My homework is done," he announced. "What are we going to talk about this time, Mom?"

Mother sat down next to Michael. "Let's talk about people who stayed faithful to Jesus in spite of all the compromises that were taking place in the Christian church. Because even with all the changes, there still were small groups of people who remembered the simple Christian truths that Jesus had taught. They taught these truths to their children. Little groups of Sabbath keepers were scattered in Europe, Central Africa, and Armenia." Mother showed Michael where these places were on a large map of the world.

"One of these groups was known as the Waldenses," she continued, "because they followed the teachings of a man named Peter Waldo. The Waldenses were persecuted by other Christians, so they went to live in the mountains, high up in the Alps. They didn't just hide in the mountains, though; they were very busy people. They were among the first people in Europe to have the Scriptures written in their own language. They called themselves the 'Church in the Wilderness.' "

"Great," said Michael, "finally some Bibles! Now people could study and see what's really true."

"Yes," said Mother, "studying the Bible was important to the Waldenses. They helped their children memorize long parts of the Old and New Testaments. Many children memorized the entire books of Matthew and John and some of the books written by the apostle Paul. When they were old enough, they copied sections of Scripture to share with others.

"The Waldenses translated the Bible into the local language so people could read and understand it. The church leaders didn't like the people having Scriptures that they could study on their own. Being able to study the Scriptures for themselves led them to ask questions and sometimes argue with the teachings of the leaders. So the Waldensian children had to hide their Scriptures. They also had to learn to be very careful what they said and to whom.

"These families did their farming on the mountainsides. They grew vegetables, and they raised sheep. They made things from the sheep's wool, and they made cheese from the milk. Some of these things they sold in the villages. As they went from house to house selling their wares, they were able to talk about the Bible with people who were interested. In their clothes, they carried a few papers on which they had written part of the Bible. In fact, the women would sew wide hems and secret pockets in their clothes in order to have places to hide portions of Scripture. Two by two, the Waldenses went out, whether they were merchants or students. They spread the Word of God like yeast, and in this way, the true teachings of the Bible would find their way throughout a whole village or school, yet the leaders couldn't figure out where they were coming from."

"Hmm," said Michael, "I'm sure glad I'm not a Waldensian kid; I'd have to memorize too many Bible texts!"

Mother laughed. "Actually," she said, "memorizing Scripture

is a very good idea. It helps exercise your mind, and you might not always have your Bible handy. The time may come when you will be very glad that you learned your memory verses for Sabbath School—and other Bible passages too."

"I guess so," said Michael.

"And think about this," said Mother. "What would it be like if you and your brother were the only ones in your school with a Bible?"

"It would be lonely," said Michael.

"Maybe," agreed Mother, "but God used boys just like you and Donnie to change entire schools. And if you let Him, He can use you for important jobs too. Today, God needs boys like you, just like He did during Waldensian times."

"I've never thought about it that way," said Michael. "I always figured God had all the grown-ups He needed and that He didn't need me until later."

"That's not true," said Mother, "God needs you now."

Michael grinned. "That's good news! I didn't want to wait until I was grown up, anyway," he said.

5

John
Wycliffe

The next day, as Mother and Michael were doing the dishes, Mother continued the story.

"In England, God used a man named John Wycliffe for a special job. Wycliffe lived during the time when Edward III was king of England—about six hundred fifty years ago. He had been educated at the university in England and had always been a serious Bible student. Later, he was the chaplain to the king of England."

"You mean, like the king's personal pastor?" asked Michael.

"Yes," replied Mother. "John Wycliffe was concerned about several things that he felt were wrong with the church at that time. The king had to pay taxes to the pope, who was the head of the Christian church. John Wycliffe didn't think he should have to do that. Wycliffe also noticed that some church leaders were lazy. They went around getting money from the people, but they didn't work for a living, and they didn't help the people who gave them money. Wycliffe called them greedy. He said it wasn't fair that they got rich while the sick and the poor had nothing. If Jesus was their example, then they should be helping people—not taking away their money."

"I bet the church leaders didn't like John Wycliffe at all," said Michael.

"You're quite right," said Mother. "They were happy when the king sent him as an ambassador to the Netherlands."

"Is that Holland?" asked Michael.

"Yes," said Mother. "Wycliffe was in Holland for two years. But after two years, he came back. Soon the church leaders tried to take him to court for heresy."

"What's heresy?" asked Michael.

"Heresy is believing and teaching things that are different from what the church teaches and believes," said Mother. "Even though the church leaders wanted to condemn Wycliffe and kill him, he had the support of two princes and many people in England. The judges were afraid to convict him, so they let him go. Wycliffe organized missionaries and sent them all through England to teach about Jesus. In Oxford, where Oxford University is, Wycliffe became known as the 'gospel doctor.' He taught there for many years.

"One time he became very sick from hard work and study. The church leaders were excited. They came and told him he was dying. They asked him if he wanted to admit now that he was wrong about what he believed and taught. He said, 'I shall not die, but live!' He still had work to do for God. And he *did* live. He got better, much to everyone's surprise.

"God kept John Wycliffe alive because he had another special job to do. Remember, Michael, that we talked about ordinary people back then not having Bibles to read? The few Bibles that existed were in Latin."

Michael interrupted, "Did the people in England speak Latin?"

"Only the educated people." said Mother. "All over Europe educated people learned Latin so they could talk together and study the same books."

"Neat!" said Michael.

MICHAEL ASKS WHY

"Bibles were handwritten," Mother continued, "because printing hadn't been invented in Europe at that time. And they were chained to the wall or desks in churches because they were so valuable.

"John Wycliffe prepared the first Bible translation in English. It had to be handwritten, too, so he had several other people make more handwritten copies. This was very slow and expensive. The hand-copied Scriptures were hard to come by, so they were split up into small parts and passed out to many families. John Wycliffe wanted every family in England to have the Bible in English so they could learn that their salvation was through Christ alone.

"Three times the church leaders tried to bring John Wycliffe to trial for heresy. And three times they were unable to do anything about it. John Wycliffe finally died in his little church. He collapsed just before they started Communion."

"That was a really good time to die," said Michael.

"Why do you say that?" asked Mother.

"Well, we were talking about Communion in my baptismal class," said Michael, "and before Communion, you are supposed to prepare your heart and confess all your sins. That means that John Wycliffe died with a clean heart, right before Communion."

Mom smiled. "Yes, that may have been a good time for him to die. But if we love Jesus and have invited Him into our heart, we know that He is with us all the time. Whenever we die, we don't have to worry if Jesus is in our heart."

"I'm really glad that John Wycliffe didn't die the first time he was so sick," said Michael. "I'm glad the Bible is in English. I don't understand Latin at all."

Mom nodded. "English has changed a lot since John Wycliffe first translated the Bible. You probably wouldn't understand his translation either. But I'm glad we have the Bible in the language we speak today so that we can read and study for ourselves."

6

Two
Heroes

"Who are we going to talk about today?" asked Michael.

"Two more special people that God gave jobs to do. They lived in Bohemia about six hundred years ago."

"Where's Bohemia?" asked Michael.

"Bohemia is part of what we call the Czech Republic today. John Huss and his friend Jerome both lived in Bohemia. John Huss's father died when John was very young. His mother dedicated John to God, just like Dad and I dedicated you to God when you were little. She asked God to look after John and to take care of him, and in return John would be His man.

"God did take care of John and helped him get a good education. When John traveled to the university in Prague, his mother went with him. She didn't have much to give her son, but as they neared the city, she knelt down and prayed that God would bless him always. And God answered her prayer. John Huss finished his education, and then he went to work in the king's court as one of the king's special priests.

MICHAEL ASKS WHY

"John's friend Jerome had traveled to England, where he met the queen of England who was a Bohemian princess. She was far away from home and probably very happy to find someone else from Bohemia to talk to. Jerome and the queen of England studied Wycliffe's writings and found them very interesting. Back home again in Bohemia, Jerome shared Wycliffe's writing with John Huss. They both became very excited about them. However, the church leaders warned them not to say anything about these new ideas.

"About this time, Huss and Jerome met two men from England who had not been allowed to preach about Wycliffe's writings either. These two men were artists, and they decided to make a picture sermon. They painted two pictures next to each other. The first was a picture of Jesus dressed very simply and riding on a donkey. Next to this picture was another painting that showed the pope sitting on his horse, wearing his triple crown and expensive flowing robes. Following him were other important church leaders and men blowing trumpets—all dressed in beautiful clothes. Without saying a word, these paintings showed the difference between Jesus, with His humble, simple ways, and the self-important, luxurious way the church leaders lived. How different they were!

"Although these two men said nothing and preached their sermon silently through their art, Huss wasn't afraid to preach out loud. He preached everywhere. It wasn't long before the church leaders were very upset. They called Huss to Rome for a trial. However, the king and queen of Bohemia protected him and asked that he not have to go to Rome. The church leaders in Rome were very angry and went ahead with the trial although Huss wasn't there! They condemned him, so he had to leave Prague for a safer place.

"At this time, Huss was not sure just what he should do. He knew there were many things in the church that were not right. Yet, he still believed that it was God's church. God was leading him little by little and teaching him one thing at a time."

"That was kind of God," said Michael. "If He had showed Huss all the church's mistakes at once, he would have felt terrible. It would have been too many things to change at one time."

"I think you're right," agreed Mother. "God treats us like that too. He teaches us one thing at a time so that it's not too much for us either.

"Again the church leaders asked Huss to come and talk with them. Everyone—the king of Bohemia, Emperor Sigismond, and even the pope—promised that Huss would be safe if he would just come. So he agreed to go to the city of Constance and talk to the church leaders. As he traveled, people flocked to see him, and he preached to everyone along the way. But when he arrived, he was thrown into a castle dungeon, on the far side of the Rhine River where he became very sick. So much for promises.

"When his friend Jerome learned what had happened to Huss, he went to Constance to try to help him. But Jerome soon found himself in prison as well.

"Finally, the church leaders brought Huss out of the dungeon. They dressed him in a priest's robe and put a big dunce's cap on his head. On the cap was written 'Arch Heretic.' Huss bowed his head and said softly, 'Jesus was wrapped in a robe that wasn't His when He was on trial. And Jesus wore a crown of thorns for me. I can wear this dunce cap for Him.'

"The leaders dragged him through the streets and tied him to a stake and set him on fire! Through all of this, Huss acted as if he were going to a wedding party. He smiled and looked very calm. When men tied him to the stake and lighted the fire, he didn't scream or cry with pain. He sang! And he continued to sing until he died.

"Meanwhile Jerome was sick and still in prison. The church leaders tried to get him to admit that he was wrong and they were right. 'Prove to me from the Bible that I am wrong,' Jerome told them, 'and I will do as you say.' Day after day, the church leaders kept trying to get Jerome to give up his faith. Finally, he had been in prison so long, and he was so discouraged by what had happened to his friend Huss, that at last he did what the church leaders asked him to do. He said he didn't agree with Huss or Wycliffe any more and that he would believe what the church leaders told him to believe.

"But the leaders still kept him in prison. As Jerome thought about what he had done, he knew that he had denied truth. He thought about how courageous Huss had been. He thought about how much Jesus had suffered for him. So he called the church leaders and told them that he was sorry he had done what they told him to do. He told them that he really did believe what the Bible said was true—even if they disagreed. The leaders were very angry, and so they took Jerome to the stake and burned him, too, just as they had Huss. Like his friend, Jerome also died singing.

"The church leaders took the ashes of Huss and Jerome and threw them into the Rhine River. They said the river would wash away all traces of these two 'heretics.' But instead, little pieces of their ashes floated along the river all the way through the whole country out to the sea and, finally, on to the entire world. And, like their ashes, the message that these two men preached eventually went to the whole world too."

"Did they really sing while they were burning?" asked Michael.

"Yes," Mother replied.

"That's a good thing to know when I'm thinking about the difficult things that will happen just before Jesus comes again," said Michael. "If Huss and Jerome were able to sing even though mean people were hurting their bodies, then that means that Jesus helped them not to feel it. And if Jesus could be with them so that they could sing until they died, then He could do that for me too."

"That's right," said Mother, "He certainly could."

7

Martin Luther

"Who are we talking about today?" asked Michael.

"Martin Luther," answered Mother. "He lived in the 1500s."

"Oh, I've heard of him," said Michael. "He wrote the song, *A Mighty Fortress Is Our God.*" Michael started to sing:

"A mighty fortress is our God,
A bulwark never failing;
Our helper He, amid the flood
Of mortal ills prevailing."

"Very good!" Mother said. "What do you think Martin Luther knew about fortresses?"

"I don't know," said Michael, "Did he live in a castle?"

"For a while," said Mother, "but it wasn't much fun. He was a prisoner in a castle, but let's start at the beginning.

"When Martin Luther went away to school, his father wanted him to be a lawyer. His parents were very poor, and for a while, Martin had to sing songs from door to door so that he could buy food with the money people gave him. Often he went to bed hungry.

MICHAEL ASKS WHY

"After two years of college, Martin Luther decided he would rather be a priest than a lawyer. His father was very angry with him. Martin's mother and father had always raised him to love God, and they had prayed for him. They just hadn't expected him to be a priest. Although his parents had more money now, his father refused to give him any money for school if he was going to become a priest. But later they changed their minds and helped him.

"Martin Luther was a good man who loved God very much. He had become more and more worried about his sins and wanted to please God and be forgiven. So he would fast."

"What, go without eating?" exclaimed Michael.

"Yes," said Mother, "and stay awake all night. Those were called vigils. He would do this to punish himself for his sins."

"That doesn't sound healthy," said Michael.

"It wasn't," said Mother. "Soon Martin Luther was sick. He became so sick that he would often faint; even after he stopped his fasts and vigils, he never fully recovered."

"That's sad," said Michael. "Didn't he know that Jesus died for him and he didn't have to do that stuff?"

"He learned," smiled Mother. "One day in a monastery . . ."

"What's a monastery?" interrupted Michael.

"It's a place where monks, priests, and church leaders live," replied Mother.

"What's a monk?" Michael wanted to know.

"A monk," said Mother, "is a special kind of priest. He takes special vows and lives with other monks in a monastery. One day when Martin Luther was living in a monastery, he saw something that delighted him. It was a Latin Bible chained to the wall. He had seen a Bible in the university and had loved to read it. Now he was fascinated to find one in the monastery. He spent every spare minute, even when he should have been eating or sleeping, reading the Latin Bible.

"As he read the Bible, Martin Luther discovered that he didn't have to fast and do other things to try to pay for his sins because

Martin Luther

Jesus had already paid for them all. He became very excited! He realized that all he needed to do was to love Jesus, have faith in Him, and obey Him.

"Not everyone was as excited as Martin Luther about this good news. A man named Tetzel was in charge of selling indulgences in Germany. Indulgences were pieces of paper that people could buy that gave them forgiveness for a sin, or sometimes for many sins. Tetzel would even sell indulgences ahead of time if you were planning to commit a sin!"

Mother laughed. "In several books I've read a really funny story about Tetzel. Once he sold an indulgence for future sins to a certain man. The next day, as Tetzel traveled through the countryside to a nearby town, that same man robbed him of all the money he had earned selling indulgences. Tetzel began to curse the thief and told him he would burn in hell for stealing his money! But the robber just grinned, pulled out the indulgence he had bought the day before, and shook it in Tetzel's face. And then he rode off with the money!"

"Wow!" exclaimed Michael. "How could Tetzel really believe in indulgences after that?"

"He probably didn't." said Mother. "Luther preached about Jesus' love for us and how He had died for us so that no one needed indulgences.

"Tetzel was very angry and complained to the church leaders. Luther tried to tell people that indulgences were worthless and unnecessary, but Tetzel kept selling them anyway. Just before a religious holiday, when lots of people would be in town and at the church, Luther nailed a paper on the church door. Written on the paper were ninety-five statements showing that indulgences and other church teachings were not what the Bible taught. Luther offered to explain these statements to everyone who would come to the church the next day.

Luther kept pointing out teachings that were not in the Bible. Many people agreed with Luther, but the church leaders became more and more angry. Finally, the pope, the head of the church, declared Martin Luther a heretic and excommunicated him and all of his followers."

"What does it mean to be excommunicated?" asked Michael.

"It means that the pope said that Martin Luther could not go to heaven and that he could not pray to God anymore and that he could not worship with other Christians anymore. If he died, he could not even be buried in the same cemetery as other Christians."

"But the pope couldn't do that," said Michael. "Only God can decide who goes to heaven."

"That's true," said Mother. "But that's what the pope said. Martin Luther had taught other things, too, that upset the church leaders. He preached against all of their extravagant palaces, feasts, robes, fancy foods, and other sins. He felt that the church leaders should lead a simple life like Jesus lived. He was brought to trial in Germany by the church leaders, and they planned to bring him to Rome. But Martin Luther escaped. God kept protecting him.

"Many people consider Martin Luther the first Protestant because he was excommunicated from the church."

"What is a Protestant?" asked Michael.

"Well," Mother answered, "when Luther lived, there really was only one Christian church. It was called the 'Catholic' church because it was the church that everyone belonged to. But Luther protested against practices and teachings in the Catholic Church that didn't follow what Jesus taught in the Bible. When he was excommunicated, he was no longer a Catholic. Those, like Luther, who protested against the Catholic Church came to be called 'Protestants.' And Luther was one of the first of these protesters.

"Actually, Martin Luther was not happy about being put out of the Catholic Church. He had meant to be a Catholic always. He wanted to correct the things that were wrong with his church, not leave it. And it made him very sad not to be part of his church anymore."

Martin Luther

"But he had to believe what the Bible said, didn't he?" Michael asked. "He couldn't just go along with his church even if it was going against the Bible."

"No, he couldn't," agreed Mother. "But he wondered sometimes if maybe he was mistaken. All the church leaders kept telling him he was wrong. Could it be that just one man was right and everyone else was wrong? But the more he read the Bible, the more sure he was that the church was wrong about many things. And so he kept on preaching and teaching what he found in the Bible. Many people in Germany began to listen to Luther and to think that he was right. This made the church leaders even more angry and afraid. They tried even harder to make Luther stop preaching and teaching."

"Why did the church leaders hate Luther so much?" asked Michael. "Why didn't they listen to him?"

"It isn't easy to admit you are wrong," Mother said. "People today often believe what they want to believe—even if it disagrees with the Bible. It was that way in Martin Luther's day, it's that way today, and it will be that way until Jesus comes."

"I wish Jesus would come right away," said Michael. "Then everyone would be happy and agree with each other."

"That will be a wonderful day," Mother said.

8

A Champion of Truth

"Whatever happened to Martin Luther?" asked Michael. "Did the church leaders stay mad at him?"

"Yes they did," said Mother. He was asked to come before a group called the Diet. They met in a place called Worms, so the council was known as the Diet of Worms."

Michael started to giggle. "It sounds like something birds would enjoy," he laughed.

"It does sound funny in English, doesn't it?" said Mom. "But, Luther spoke German, so he didn't think it was funny, and especially, he didn't think it was funny at all having to go to Worms. But he didn't have a choice. Charles V was the emperor, and he commanded Luther to come. It was a two-week trip. Luther was sick and needed help getting there. It was a long trip, and he talked to everyone along the way. At one stop, a friendly priest held up a picture of an Italian man who had been killed for being a heretic."

"That's called a martyr, isn't it?" asked Michael.

"Right," said Mother. "One of the men traveling with Luther

was concerned that he would be discouraged and asked him if he wanted to go forward. Luther answered, 'Even if I am chased out of every city, I shall go on.'

"Later they came to a city called Erfurt, where Luther had many friends. His friends came out to honor him, and he preached to all of them. This was the same city that he had come through as a beggar, many years before. Now he was a famous preacher, and the people were excited to have him back. Many of them were very worried about him. One of them called out, 'They will burn you and reduce your body to ashes as they did with John Huss.' But Martin Luther replied, 'Even if they should build a fire all the way from Wittenberg to Worms, I would still walk through the flames and appear before the council in order to testify to the Word of God.'

"By the time Luther and his group got to the city of Worms, a big crowd was waiting to welcome them. It was much larger than the crowd that had come out to welcome the emperor. Some church leaders wanted to burn Luther at the stake right away, without even letting him speak or without listening to what he had to say. But the emperor said 'No, let him speak.'

"When the council met, Luther spoke respectfully to the church leaders and about the church. He confessed that some of the things he had written were not as courteous as they should have been. Luther had a quick temper and had written some angry things about the church leaders at times. But he also told the council that unless the church leaders could show him from the Scriptures where he was wrong, he would not take back anything that he had said. The church leaders were not able to do that.

"The council gave Luther one more chance to admit he was wrong and take back the things he had preached and taught. But he refused to change his mind. He made a powerful speech explaining that he had to believe the Bible. He ended by saying, 'Here I stand, I can do nothing else. May God help me.'

"The leaders kept him there in Worms. Many princes, counts,

barons, and other important people visited him. He had so many visitors that his little room could not hold them all. Finally the council let him go. The trip home from Worms was long, but many people honored him along the way.

"Luther still had enemies that wanted to kill him. Frederick of Saxony, a ruler who helped protect Luther, was worried about his safety. He was sure the church leaders would find a way to kill Martin Luther on his trip home, so he sent his own men to 'kidnap' him. Frederick's soldiers brought Luther to Frederick's castle at Wartburg. There Luther lived like a prisoner for his own safety and protection. However, he didn't waste his time while at the castle. He began to translate the New Testament into German so the people in his country could read the Bible in their own language. He also wrote many letters to encourage Christians everywhere to keep their eyes on Jesus.

"Some people felt that the reformation of the church was Luther's special job and that it started and ended with Luther. This isn't true. The church will continue to be reformed until Jesus comes. Luther's job was to show others the things that God had shown him. Yet, God didn't show him everything. God teaches us one thing at a time; then, as we are able to learn more, He teaches us new things. Martin Luther's followers formed a church which is known today as the Lutheran Church."

"Oh," said Michael, "we know some Lutherans!"

"Yes, we do," Mother said. "They are people who follow the teachings of Martin Luther."

"Well, what about the other things that people learned later?"

"We'll talk about those things tomorrow," said Mother.

"Wow!" said Michael. "Now I know where Orthodox people, Catholic people, and Lutherans came from."

9

Ulric Zwingli

"Do we have another Reformation hero to talk about today?" asked Michael.

"We sure do," Mother replied. "Today, our hero's name is Zwingli. When Zwingli was thirteen years old, he was sent to Berne, Switzerland."

"Thirteen?" said Michael. "That's only a little bit older than I am!"

"That's right," Mother agreed.

"That's pretty young to be sent away from home," Michael said.

"Yes," said Mother, "it is. Zwingli was sent to a well-respected school where he could learn to be a speaker and a writer. He also studied music and poetry. But after a while, his family became concerned that the church leaders would convince him to join a monastery, so eventually his father asked him to come home again. Later, Zwingli studied in the city of Basel and learned about God's free forgiveness.

MICHAEL ASKS WHY

"When Zwingli became a pastor, he started preaching things that he had learned from studying the Scriptures. He preached that grace was a free gift and that people didn't have to earn their salvation. He was also studying the Greek and Hebrew Scriptures and translating them into the local language and sharing his translation with the people.

"The people asked him, 'Are you doing what Luther is doing? Are you a follower of Luther?'

" 'I don't even know Luther,' said Zwingli. 'But if he is preaching Christ, then he is doing what I'm doing!'

"At a town called Einsiedeln was a statue of the Virgin Mary that many believed worked miracles. People traveled from all over Europe to visit it, hoping for special miracles to happen for themselves. Zwingli was invited to be the minister at Einsiedeln. He stood right beside the image and preached that no one received forgiveness except through Jesus. Some people who heard him were very angry to think that there was no reason for their trip to the statue. Others were excited. Although some people were very happy to hear Zwingli's message, it meant that fewer visitors came to visit the shrine of the Virgin Mary. So there was less money for the people who lived there, and Zwingli earned less money too."

"But still, Zwingli must have been pleased that people were learning the truth from the Bible," Michael interrupted.

"I'm sure he was," said Mother. "Later he became a preacher at the Zurich cathedral. There, he was supposed to collect money for the cathedral from sick people who were hoping their donations would make them better, from sinners who gave large offerings wanting to be forgiven, and from people who wanted to show their love for the church by giving lots of money.

"Zwingli began to notice that some of the church leaders were willing to give Communion only to important people; they wouldn't let the poor people have Communion at all. It seemed that for many pastors, collecting money and giving Communion to important people was a substitute for preaching. How do you think Zwingli fit in with a job like that?"

"I bet he showed them some *real* preaching," said Michael.

"You're right," agreed Mother. "Zwingli said, 'I will preach the life of Christ and the gospel of Matthew.' And that's what he did. He made many people angry. A man named Samson, who was in charge of selling indulgences in that area, had to leave because no one would buy his indulgences any more after hearing Zwingli preach.

"During the year 1519, a terrible plague came through Europe. It was called the Great Death, because so many people died. The rumor started going around that Zwingli had died too, but it wasn't true. God still had work for him to do. Zwingli was sick, but he recovered and continued preaching. But instead of telling people how bad they were and asking them for money so they could be forgiven, Zwingli told them of Jesus' love for them. The people were so happy to hear Zwingli's sermons. He told them the wonderful Bible stories about Jesus and His teachings.

"This made the church leaders more and more angry with Zwingli. They had a trial in the city of Baden, and Zwingli was put out of the church. This made him very sad, but he still continued preaching. Zwingli was a great encouragement to those who were discouraged by Martin Luther's disappearance. Even though Martin Luther was safe, hiding in the castle at Wartburg, many of his friends didn't know where he was. They were afraid that he was in jail or maybe even dead."

"They should have known that God was watching out for Luther all along," said Michael. "God wouldn't let anybody die if they still had work to do. Look at Wycliffe and Zwingli. God took care of them; He could take care of Martin Luther too."

"Yes, that's true," said Mother, "and it's an important thing for us to remember today and in the future."

10

Progress and Difficulties

"It must have been hard on Luther's friends, not knowing where he was or how he was doing," observed Michael.

"Yes," answered Mother. "Martin Luther's friends became more and more worried about him. There were rumors that he had been killed. At first, the church leaders were glad that Luther's friends were so discouraged, but soon they became frightened because Luther's followers were becoming more and more angry. Finally, people heard the news that Luther was safe, and this calmed the anger."

"His friends must have been so glad to know he was alive and all right," said Michael.

"They were," Mother replied. "They read his writings even more eagerly than before. Satan couldn't crush Luther by making things hard on him, so now the devil tried to destroy him and his teachings by deceiving some of Luther's followers. They began arguing among themselves. One man even claimed that he had received instructions from the angel Gabriel. The leaders of the

Progress and Difficulties

Catholic Church were happy as they watched the Protestants become more and more confused. Could this be the end of the Reformation?

"Luther left the castle at Wartburg and started preaching to make things clearer to his friends. 'You were led by the spirit, but which spirit?' he asked. The people had to think. Was it the Holy Spirit?"

"I don't think so," answered Michael. "The Holy Spirit doesn't cause people to become false prophets and to argue with each other!"

"Right," agreed Mother. "The church in Wittenberg was packed and overflowing when Luther stood up to preach. Luther spoke against violence. Many of his followers had been angry and violent toward other church members and toward the Catholics. Luther said this was wrong. Christians should not be violent against each other."

"Luther was right!" commented Michael.

"Luther said, 'God does more by His word alone than you or I and all the world can do by united strength.' Martin Luther had other problems to deal with. Some of his followers were now speaking against order in worship. They believed church members should just be led by the Spirit and that this meant they could worship any way they felt like worshiping."

"Wouldn't that be terribly noisy and distracting?" Michael wanted to know. "It sounds irreverent to me."

"Martin Luther thought so too. He brought back order in his church services. Some of his followers even burned Bibles, saying 'The letter of the law kills, but the spirit brings life.'"

"But without Bibles, how would they know what was really true? How would they know what was right or wrong?" asked Michael. "Burning Bibles was a bad idea."

"That's what Luther thought too," said Mother. "Luther reminded them that without the Scriptures they would have no safeguard and nothing by which to judge what was truth and what was not. 'We have to live by the Scriptures alone,' said Luther.

"Again and again, Martin Luther had to warn his followers about their violence. They actually fought against the leaders of the Catholic Church, and many people were killed. Luther told them that the only weapon they should be using in this war was the sword of the Spirit (the Bible). 'Rather than see our gospel cause one drop of blood to be shed,' Luther said, 'we should rather die ten times ourselves.' The church leaders blamed all the fighting on Luther, even though he worked so hard to stop it.

"In spite of all these things, God still had everything under control. Luther had completed the translation of the New Testament, a tremendous gift for the German-speaking people. Now they could study Jesus' words for themselves and discuss Bible truth with their church leaders. Ordinary people, and even children, came to know and understand the Bible better than many priests and other church leaders. Later, Luther started translating the Old Testament."

"Is violence and fighting always wrong?" asked Michael.

"Christians shouldn't fight and hurt each other," said Mother, "and they shouldn't fight and hurt other people either."

"A Christian soldier," said Michael, "should just use the sword of the Spirit and the shield of faith, right?"

"That's right," said Mother. "The armor and weapons of the Christian are his knowledge of the Bible and his faith in Jesus."

"That's the kind of soldier I want to be," said Michael.

11

Trusting God

"Are we still talking about Luther?" Michael asked.

"Yes," answered Mother. "In 1529 the emperor, Charles V, called a group of church leaders together to have a meeting. This group was called the Diet of Spires. Luther was not allowed to come, so he sent some friends to represent him. The church leaders declared that everyone must accept the authority of the Catholic Church and be under its control. There could be no new Lutherans. People who had already decided to follow Luther's teachings could continue to do so, but they could not preach or teach or try to tell anyone else about their beliefs.

"The people at the Diet of Spires thought about this. If everyone was in one church except a few Lutherans who didn't talk to others about what they believed, there would be no more fighting. No more people would be killed, and there would be peace. But would the Lutherans be able to follow their conscience? Was it right to forbid people to believe the Bible the way they understood it? Or to follow its teachings as they thought best? It came to a vote, and the people at the meeting were split half and half.

"The princes of Germany were present at the Diet of Spires, and they were the ones who voted. Up until now, the princes of Germany had been able to choose how they believed. Now the church leaders wanted all of the princes to believe the same way and belong to the Catholic Church. It was a difficult decision to make. One man said, 'This rule would make us choose between denying the Word of God or being burned.' Another said, 'We will obey the emperor in everything as long as it helps keep peace and honors God.'"

"But they couldn't honor God and still obey the church leaders," said Michael.

"That's right," said Mother. "The church leaders were at first amazed, and then upset and alarmed as they realized that many of the Lutherans were deciding to obey God rather than them.

"Luther's friend Melanchthon had been at the Diet of Spires. Now he was hurrying home through the streets near the Rhine River. Suddenly, a solemn, old man he had never seen before approached him. 'In a minute,' the old man told him, 'officers will be sent to arrest Grynaeus.' Quickly Melanchthon found his friend Grynaeus and helped him escape across the river. When Melanchthon returned to the city, he found that officers had searched Grynaeus's house and had torn it apart from top to bottom looking for him. Once again, God had everything under control."

"Good for God!" exclaimed Michael.

"The next year, another meeting was held, this time in Augsburg. Once again, Luther could not attend, but he traveled part of the way to Augsburg with his friends. Luther cheered the people by singing his fortress song."

"The same fortress song we know?" asked Michael.

"Yes," answered Mother. "The people sang along with Luther and were encouraged. But the church leaders were unhappy. One of them admitted, 'All that the Lutherans have said is true; we cannot deny it.'

"Someone asked, 'Do you have good arguments to show that Luther's friends are wrong in what they believe and teach?'

"A church scholar answered, 'Not from the writings of the apostles and the prophets of the Bible, but there are arguments we can find in the writings of the church fathers and councils.'

" 'Then,' responded the questioner, 'according to you, the Lutherans agree with the Scriptures, and we don't.'

"During these discouraging times, God was still protecting his faithful people. Luther spent much time in prayer. He knew Satan was trying hard to destroy the truth of the gospel. During the meeting at Augsburg, Luther spent at least three hours a day praying! 'We can do more by praying,' he said, 'than all our enemies can do by their boasting.'

"When Luther's friend Melanchthon became discouraged, Martin wrote him a note. It said, 'God lives; He reigns; what fear then can we have?' Luther knew that if he trusted God, he didn't have to worry about what others were doing."

"If we are like Martin Luther," said Michael, "and pray and believe just what the Bible says, then we won't have anything to worry about either, will we?" asked Michael.

"You are absolutely right!" agreed Mother.

12

Light Comes
to France

"Of course, God didn't make Luther responsible for the entire continent of Europe," said Mother.

"That's good," replied Michael, "because Europe is pretty big!"

Mom chuckled. "Yes, it is. In the different countries God used different people. In France, even before Luther started preaching, God chose a man named Lefevre to spread the truth."

"Who was this Lefevre?" asked Michael.

"Lefevre was a professor at the University of Paris and a very devout Roman Catholic. He was a very intelligent man and had spent his life studying the saints and martyrs of the church. He decided to do research in the manuscripts of the Bible to find out more about the saints."

"The Bible doesn't say much about Catholic saints, does it?" Michael wanted to know. "Didn't most of them live after Bible times?"

"You're right," Mom said. "Lefevre didn't find much in the Bible about the Catholic saints, but he did find a lot of other information that made a big impression on him. He decided that a person could be saved only through faith in God and not by anything he could do himself. Lefevre shared these truths with his students, and many of them believed.

"William Farel was one of Dr. Lefevre's students. He also was very interested in the stories about the saints. He was a lot like Saul in the New Testament—very loyal to his church and quick to judge and persecute anyone who went against what he believed. But when William Farel learned the things that Dr. Lefevre had been studying, he accepted them as the truth. While Dr. Lefevre preached the truth to other students at the University of Paris, William Farel felt it was his job to teach the public in France."

"That makes sense," said Michael. "God must have given each man a group of people to teach, since there was too much work for one person."

"God is good about that," replied Mother. "About the same time, another Christian, the bishop of Meaux, discovered the truths found in the Bible. He shared them with other priests, and soon these priests were teaching the Scriptures to the French peasants around the countryside.

"But it wasn't only the peasants that were excited about what the Bible taught. Princess Margaret, sister of the king of France, also supported the bishop of Meaux and his teaching. Even King Francis I seemed interested sometimes, although he was easily influenced by his advisors, and it was hard for him to make up his mind about supporting the new teachings."

"Why did he have a hard time making up his own mind?" Michael wondered.

"Because kings have so many people putting pressure on them one way or another. And you have to remember that the church leaders were very powerful in Europe in those days," said Mother.

"Another man God called to help with the Reformation was a man named Louis de Berquin. Born a nobleman, Louis was a French knight, but he became a brave preacher of the Protestant Reformation. Some of the people in France referred to him as the second Luther. However, the Catholic Church leaders said he was even worse than Luther."

"I'll bet Luther didn't think that was a compliment," exclaimed Michael.

Mother laughed. "Three times the church leaders had Louis arrested and thrown into prison. Yet each time King Francis let him out again.

"Louis de Berquin's friend Erasmus was a famous intellectual, but he was not very brave when it came to having to choose between truth or suffering for the truth. He wrote to Louis, 'Please ask the king to send you as an ambassador to some country where you will be safe. But don't trust the king, and please don't embarrass me with your strange ideas.' "

"That sounds a little cowardly, all right" said Michael, "but I can understand why he was afraid."

"Well, Louis didn't follow Erasmus's advice. He didn't try to leave France; he just preached harder," Mother went on. "He found twelve teachings of the church that were opposed to what the Bible taught. He presented these to the people and called on the king to judge which were true—the Bible or the teachings of the church.

"Now the church leaders were scared and angry. What if the king decided Louis was right? Just before the king was to give his decision, a statue of the Virgin Mary was knocked down and broken in Paris. 'This is the work of de Berquin's followers,' the people shouted and had him arrested."

"It wasn't de Berquin's fault, was it?" asked Michael.

"No," answered Mother, "but it was an excuse to arrest him. The king left Paris for the weekend and did not stay to defend Louis. They took Louis to trial early that morning and had him executed by noon. Louis went to his death wearing his very best clothes and didn't look unhappy at all.

"Back at Meaux, the bishop's followers were not allowed to

teach anymore. So, they left Meaux and traveled all over Europe, preaching as they went."

"But that way the message was spread even farther instead of being stopped," observed Michael.

"Yes," replied Mother. "Lefevre went to Germany, and William Farel went home to eastern France. He knew he would be safer there. About this time, another young Frenchman was called to work for God too."

"What was his name?" asked Michael.

"John Calvin. John had been educated as a priest. However, he had a cousin who was a Protestant. John listened carefully to what his cousin said and thought about it for a long time. Then one day he watched a heretic (a Protestant) be burned at the stake."

"That must have been awful!" exclaimed Michael.

"I'm sure it was," replied Mother. "Calvin became convinced that the Protestant message was true. He left Paris and went to live in a small town where he went from home to home giving Bible studies to the people who lived there. Later, he returned to Paris and gave house-to-house Bible studies to anyone who was interested.

"For a time, King Francis left Paris, so Princess Margaret opened up the palace to the Protestants. They set up a chapel in a room in the palace, and soon Protestant preachers were preaching there. Many people came to hear them. When he returned, the king even allowed several Protestant churches to be built, and for two years Protestants were able to preach to any French people who wanted to hear. Then, Francis changed his mind," Mother said.

"Again?"

"Again! And he closed the churches. Calvin, who thought he was safe, was praying in his room. Some friends came by and banged on the door.

" 'Calvin! Calvin! Run for safety!' they said. 'The officers are at the door to arrest you!'

"Calvin jumped up. While his friends talked to the officers at the door, Calvin climbed out the window and escaped to safety in the territories governed by Princess Margaret.

"For some time, John Calvin preached in a cave located in the side of a steep gorge where his listeners could hide under the trees and overhanging rocks if they needed to."

"Good idea!" said Michael.

Mother nodded. "Protestants in France wanted very badly for their country to become completely Protestant as had Switzerland and Germany. They put up posters all over France, describing how bad they thought the Catholic mass was. One poster even appeared on the door of the king's private room!"

"That must have made him really mad," Michael grinned.

"King Francis was furious. He led his city in the execution of as many Protestants as possible. They captured a poor Protestant and tortured him until he agreed to show them where other Protestants lived. They walked through the streets. Each time he stopped in front of a Protestant home, the soldiers would rush in and arrest the family and bring them out. The Protestants were tied to stakes and burned. But they went to the stake joyfully, just as Huss and Jerome had done in Bohemia because they knew God loved them."

"That was very brave!" said Michael.

Mother nodded. "The soldiers accused the Protestants of planning to kill all the Catholics, of planning to overthrow the government, and of planning to murder the king. And even though there was no evidence for this, the French people were furious that anyone would think of committing such crimes.

"On January 21, 1535, the king led a parade through Paris. All of the loyal Catholic Church members were to light a torch in their doorway. Scaffolds and stakes were set up all along the way, with Protestants tied to them, and as the king reached each one, they were set on fire. It was a terrible, terrible day. France had turned its back on the light God was trying to send it.

Light Comes to France

"Another king of France would be taken through the streets of Paris 258 years later on the same day—January 21—and executed. And not only he but 2,800 other people would die during the French Revolution."

"How horrible!" Michael exclaimed.

"It would be just another example of what happened because France turned its back on God's Word."

"What happened to William Farel and John Calvin? asked Michael. "Did they get killed?"

"No," answered Mother. "William Farel and John Calvin escaped to Switzerland, where they worked hard and faced many dangers. They finally turned the city of Geneva into a sort of refuge for Reformers from all over Europe. Much later Calvin's followers established the Presbyterian Church."

"Oh, we know some Presbyterians," exclaimed Michael. "Dr. Germroth comes to your Friday night Bible study group."

"Yes, he and his family are loyal Presbyterians."

"There sure were a lot of churches that started during the Reformation, and we have friends in all of them," said Michael.

"You are right," said Mother. "God was working to bring His people back to a clearer understanding of Himself."

13

God's Heroes in Scandinavia

"Today," announced Mother, "we're going to talk about heroes for the truth in the Netherlands and Scandinavia."

"Scandinavia means Norway and Sweden, doesn't it?" Michael asked.

"I think it includes Denmark and Finland too," answered Mother. "In Holland, God called a man named Menno Simons to teach the truth to the Dutch people. At first, Menno Simons was afraid to read the Bible because he didn't want to be tricked into 'heresy.' When he felt an urge to study the Bible, he thought it was a temptation from Satan! Imagine that! But finally, after he started reading the German New Testament that Luther had translated and some of Luther's other writings, he became convinced that Luther was right.

"He started studying the Bible to find out more about baptism and why people should be baptized as babies instead of as adults."

"That's not what we believe, is it?" asked Michael.

Mother smiled. "Simons couldn't find anything about babies

being baptized anywhere in the Bible. He did find in the Bible that adults were baptized when they chose to follow Jesus. He decided that perhaps the 'heretics' were right."

"They were," commented Michael.

"At that time, there were two groups of Protestants in Holland. One group was descended from the Waldenses. You remember, Michael, how we talked about the Waldenses and how they lived in the Alps and remained faithful to God?"

"I remember," said Michael.

"Good," replied Mother. "The other group of Protestant Christians in Holland thought the only way to bring about change was through violence and fighting. They were fanatics. This fanatical group caused a lot of problems for the other Christians. Both in the Netherlands and in northern Germany, the followers of Menno Simons were sometimes confused with these fanatical Protestants. The authorities passed laws against all of them. In Holland, it became a capital crime to read the Bible or even to hear it read—to preach it or even talk about it!"

"What is a capital crime?" asked Michael.

"A capital crime," answered Mother," is any crime for which you can be put to death. Not only could people not read or listen to the Bible, but they could be put to death for praying in secret, refusing to bow down to an image, or for singing a psalm.

"When people were caught doing any of those things—even if they confessed and agreed not to do those things anymore, they were still put to death. However, the Protestants in Holland were brave; whole families stuck together—husbands, wives, and children. They were not afraid to stand up for what they believed."

"They must have prayed that God would end the persecution soon!" exclaimed Michael.

"Yes, and God answered their prayers," said Mother. "Before long, William of Orange led the Protestant Revolution and became king of Holland. Holland was now a Protestant country.

"Meanwhile, in Denmark, God used a man named Tausen.

MICHAEL ASKS WHY

He was born as a peasant's son."

"God used a lot of poor people, didn't he?" commented Michael.

Mother nodded. "Peasants were not able to provide their children with education, yet young Tausen was bright and eager to learn, so he joined a monastery. The monks realized he was very intelligent. They were willing to send him to school for more education, as long as he did not go to Wittenberg. That was where the 'heretics' were preaching their Protestant doctrines.

"Tausen went to school in Cologne, Germany. But while he was there, he learned the Protestant doctrines and moved to Wittenberg. When he went back to Denmark, the monks were furious and confined him to a cell. But instead of hiding away in a damp cell where no one ever heard his words again, he made use of this time by preaching to his fellow monks. Soon many of them were going out all over Denmark and telling others the good news."

"Their plan backfired," chuckled Michael.

"While he was there in the cell, he also translated the New Testament into Danish, so that the Danish people could read the Scriptures in their own language. Denmark accepted the reformed faith and became a Protestant country."

"What about Sweden?" asked Michael.

"In Sweden, God called two brothers, Olaf and Laurentius Petri. Their father was a blacksmith. And although they did not come from a wealthy family, they both had studied with Luther and Melanchthon while at school in Wittenberg. Olaf and Laurentius were much like Luther and Melanchthon. Olaf was a fiery preacher like Luther, and Laurentius was a deep thinker like Melanchthon. Together they spread the word in Sweden.

"Olaf was attacked by mobs several times but escaped and was protected by the king. He declared, 'The church has no authority when it goes against God's word. We should go by what the Bible says.' The king of Sweden accepted his preaching, and most of the whole country followed the king's example.

"While all this was happening, Laurentius translated the New

Testament into Swedish. The king was so pleased he commissioned the brothers to finish translating the whole Bible for the Swedish people.

"For a long time, all of northern Europe had been persecuted for trying to have freedom of choice. Now, because of Sweden's example, religious freedom in Germany and other Protestant countries became stronger."

"I guess our decisions really can affect others," said Michael.

Mother nodded. "It makes a big difference when we remember that."

14

Standing for God in England

"While Luther was busy translating the New Testament into German, Tyndale was in England, translating it into English," Mother told Michael. The dishes were done and so was Michael's homework. Once again, they were talking about how God's truth had come down through the years and how He had protected both His people and the truths they were discovering.

"But what about Wycliffe?" asked Michael. "I thought Wycliffe had already translated the Bible into English."

"Yes," said Mother, "he did. But when Tyndale translated the Bible, about two hundred years had passed since Wycliffe's work. Besides, Wycliffe's translation had been only handwritten. Now printing presses could make Bibles available to more people less expensively. Also, Wycliffe had translated the New Testament from Latin, but the New Testament had originally been written in Greek. Tyndale wanted to translate it directly from the Greek instead of translating a translation. That way it would be less likely to have mistakes in it."

Standing for God in England

"That's a good idea," said Michael. "A copy of an original should be more accurate than a copy of a copy."

"You're right," said Mother. "But the church leaders objected; they told Tyndale that only the official church could explain the Bible correctly. Tyndale replied, 'Do you know who teaches the eagles to find their prey? Well, the same God teaches His children to find their Father in His Word.' Tyndale was also famous for saying 'The Jews praised God in their own language [Hebrew, in which the Old Testament was written], and here in England, we should be able to praise Him in our own language too [by being able to read His Word in English].' Once when a highly-educated man was arguing that the common people needed the *church's* word more than *God's* Word, Tyndale vowed, 'If God spares my life, the plow boys will know more of the Scriptures than you do.'

"Tyndale faced a lot of persecution in England, and he had to leave his home. He moved to London, but soon the church leaders found him there and persecuted him more. He left and moved to Germany. In Germany, he started work on printing the New Testament in English. Several times the authorities made him stop, and he had to take his translation to another city and continue printing there. Eventually he ended up in the city of Worms where Martin Luther had been on trial. There the persecution stopped.

"He printed three thousand copies of the New Testament in his first successful printing of the English Bible. These sold so quickly that Tyndale had to do another printing the same year! These Bibles were smuggled into England by boat. The bishop of Durham was eager to keep the Bibles away from the common people. He bought a booksellers entire stock of Bibles, planning to destroy them. Tyndale made so much money from the Bibles the bishop bought that he was able to print even more Bibles than before!

"Eventually Tyndale was betrayed and thrown into prison. In prison, when he was being questioned, his jailers demanded the names of the people who had helped him with his work. Tyndale said, 'The bishop of Durham was my biggest helper; he paid a large price for my Bibles, which gave me the courage to go on with the work!' "

Michael laughed. "The bishop of Durham must have been really upset and embarrassed to hear that!"

"I'm sure he was," Mother agreed. "God works things out in mysterious ways, but He also has a tremendous sense of humor!"

"I'm glad God has a sense of humor," said Michael.

"I am too," said Mother. "Finally Tyndale was killed. He was yet another one of the special martyrs whom God will honor in heaven someday."

"I can't wait to meet him," said Michael.

"That would be fun," agreed Mother. "When Tyndale died, other people wanted to step in and take his place. Instead of one man working to spread the Bible to people in England, now there were several—Mr. Barnes, Mr. Frith, the Ridley family, and Mr. Cranmer all took over his job."

"So," said Michael, "when Tyndale died, more people than before started doing the same work. That must have made the church leaders angry."

"Yes," said Mother, "it did, but they couldn't do much about it. The work was also spreading in Scotland. Some of Wycliffe's followers had gone there as missionaries. They were called the Lollards."

"That's a funny name," said Michael.

"Well," said Mom, "they were called Lollards because the official church accused them of being lazy and lolling around all the time. Later, another missionary came to Scotland. His name was John Knox. John Knox had not intended to become a minister. When people first asked him to preach, he was shy and afraid. No way could he do that, he thought. But once he made up his mind to be a preacher for the Lord, he was never shy and afraid again. He was one of God's most outspoken ministers.

"Mary, the queen of Scotland, charged John Knox with her-

Standing for God in England

esy, but John continued to preach to her. Mary was confused. 'You teach things one way,' she said, 'and the church teaches it another. Whom shall I believe?' John Knox told her she should believe God and His Word. But she wouldn't do that, and she never did change. She died a Catholic, but her son, James, was a Protestant, and Scotland did finally become a Protestant country. Years later, when James was the king of England and Scotland, he ordered a new translation of the Bible that we still call the King James Version."

"I have a King James Bible beside my bed!" said Michael.

"Meanwhile," continued Mother, "John Bunyan was another preacher in England."

"I've heard of him," said Michael. "He wrote *Pilgrim's Progress.* That was one of my favorite books when I was little."

"That was a shortened children's edition with lots of pictures," said Mother. "The book that John Bunyan actually wrote was much longer."

"Well, he had a great imagination," said Michael, "I just love that book."

Mother chuckled. "John Bunyan was a very busy preacher for the Lord. But he got thrown into the Bedford jail. While he was in jail, he had time to write the book. In fact, if he hadn't been thrown in jail, he might never have written *Pilgrim's Progress.* Maybe being in jail was part of God's plan for John Bunyan so that all of us could read that book and learn from it.

"A hundred years later, two brothers, John and Charles Wesley, lived in England and became preachers. They went to America as missionaries to preach to people about Jesus. On the way, they found themselves on a boat with many Moravians."

"Who?" asked Michael.

"Moravians were German Christians who came from a part of Europe called Moravia," said Mother. "They were descended from people who had heard the gospel from John Huss. They were Protestants and practiced a very simple religion. They tried to live the way Jesus and His disciples had lived.

MICHAEL ASKS WHY

"On the way to America, a terrible storm came up. The captain of the ship was scared, and John Wesley was terrified. But John noticed that the Moravians didn't seem afraid at all! They sat together singing until the storm was over. The Wesley brothers were impressed with their calm faith.

"The Moravians set a good example of trust in God. They trusted God so much that it didn't matter to them whether they lived or died in the storm as long as they were in God's hands. Because of this experience John and Charles Wesley grew in their walk with Jesus."

"But they were already ministers," said Michael.

"But even ministers and people God has called to do His work can still grow and become closer to Him."

"I guess so," Michael looked thoughtful.

"The people who followed John and Charles Wesley's teachings became known as Methodists. John and Charles Wesley were very methodical in their personal devotional life and taught their followers to be the same. At first, 'Methodist' was an insulting name given to them. But soon everyone knew them as Methodists, and they even called themselves Methodists."

"There are lots of Methodists in our neighborhood," said Michael.

"Yes," said Mother, "we have many Methodist friends. Did you know that Ellen White was a Methodist?"

"She was?" asked Michael.

"Yes," said Mother. "Ellen White was baptized as a Methodist when she was eleven years old, and she remained a Methodist until she heard William Miller preach. Then she and her family followed the Millerites, who were expecting Jesus to come."

"We haven't gotten to that part of the story yet, have we?" asked Michael.

"No," said Mother, "but it's coming soon. John and Charles Wesley were often persecuted. After spending some time in America, they returned to England. There, their meetings were often interrupted by mobs, and John Wesley was chased and roughed up.

"Once, God sent an angel to protect John Wesley. The mob was reaching out and grabbing at him. One man even ripped the flap off his waistcoat, and another one ripped out a pocket that had some money in it. The money was torn in half. But when God sent the angel, the angry men just fell back and weren't able to hurt John Wesley at all.

"A big man reached out to hit John in the head. Instead, when his hand reached John Wesley's head, the tight fist opened up, and the man just ran his fingers through John's hair saying, 'Oh! What soft hair Mr. Wesley has!'

"Another time a big man did hit John Wesley in the chest and punched him in the mouth. Blood spurted from John's mouth, but he didn't seem to notice. Later, he said he hadn't felt any pain even though his mouth bled. He said it felt like somebody had tapped him with a little straw."

"Wow!" said Michael. "God really protects His people, doesn't He?"

"God often protected the Wesleys," replied Mother. "And John and Charles learned to trust Him whether or not they got hurt because they knew that God was in control, always."

"That is really neat," said Michael.

"The mobs hunted down some of John and Charles Wesley's followers too," said Mother. "Any time people faithfully follow Jesus, Satan does whatever He can to make it hard for them."

"But we can be just as faithful as the Wesley brothers, can't we?" asked Michael.

"Yes," answered Mother. "And Jesus will help us. Besides preaching, the Wesley brothers wrote many hymns. John didn't write as many as Charles, since he spent more time preaching. But Charles wrote over a thousand hymns."

"That's a lot of hymns," said Michael. "There aren't even a thousand hymns in our hymnal. We must have left out a few."

MICHAEL ASKS WHY

"Our hymnal does have nineteen hymns written by Charles and two by John," said Mother. "One of my favorites is 'O for a Thousand Tongues to Sing.' Charles Wesley wrote that one."

Michael laughed. "What would I do with a thousand tongues?" he asked.

Mother laughed too. "Michael, don't be silly! Charles Wesley probably meant that even if he did have a thousand tongues, it still wouldn't be enough to praise God for all the wonderful things He has done for us."

"Oh," said Michael. "That makes a little more sense."

"Charles also wrote, 'Jesus, Lover of My Soul' and 'Gentle Jesus, Meek and Mild.' "

Michael thought awhile. "I hope that God uses me as He did John and Charles Wesley—or maybe like John Bunyan. I think I'd like to be a writer like he was."

"Well," said Mother, "God may very well use you to do just that. But I hope that He gives you a more comfortable place to write your books than the Bedford jail!"

"I hope so too," said Michael. "But I'm going to work for God anyway, no matter where I end up."

"I'm sure that God is really happy to hear that," said Mother smiling. It looked like she was happy to hear that too!

15

France Turns Away From God

A few nights later, Michael and Mother were ready to pick up the story of the great struggle between God's truth and Satan's efforts to keep it from spreading.

"Let's talk tonight about what happened in France during this time," suggested Mother.

"Did France finally become Protestant?" Michael wanted to know.

"France had made its choice, and it chose to go against the Bible," said Mother. "The church in France made war on God's Word. For a thousand years the church had tried to keep the people from reading the Bible in their own language. So the people really didn't know much about the Bible at all. As a result, they supported the Catholic Church against the Protestant Reformation.

"In Revelation 11:2-11, the Bible talks about a period of forty-two months, or 1,260 days—actually representing 1,260 years—as a time of persecution when two witnesses would be working for God."

"Wait," exclaimed Michael. "1,260 *days* is a lot less than 1,260 *years*."

Mother smiled. "Was I getting ahead of you there? Several times in the Bible, God gave prophecies in which one day equaled one year in human time. Bible scholars study the 1,260-day prophecy with the help of the Holy Spirit. They find that the prophecy about 1,260 days describes a period of 1,260 *years*—the time from A.D. 538 to A.D. 1798."

"What was going on in those years?" asked Michael.

"The Church of Rome got control over all Christians in A.D. 538. For 1,260 years the church persecuted those who disagreed with its teachings and practices. However, in 1798, at the end of the 1,260 years, the pope was taken prisoner and died far from home. That ended the absolute power of the Roman Church. Fortunately, in some countries, the Reformation brought an end to persecution even before the end of the 1,260 years."

"God's people must have been relieved," commented Michael. "They must have been praying for the persecution to end."

"In Matthew 24:22, Jesus said the time would be shortened. How kind God was to shorten the time of persecution!" said Mother.

"But who were the two witnesses who lived 1,260 years?" asked Michael. "I thought Methuselah was the oldest man who ever lived. Wasn't he 969 years old when he died?"

"The two witnesses that John was talking about in the book of Revelation weren't actual people. They were the Old Testament and the New Testament. Christians who had wanted to make these two books available to people in their own language, so they could read and study the Word of God for themselves, were hunted and betrayed. Some were tortured. Some were left to die in dungeon cells in the bottoms of castles. Others fled to the mountains and hid in caves."

"Doesn't John talk about a 'beast' that fights against the two witnesses?" asked Michael. "Is that beast the Catholic Church?"

"No," said Mother. "The beast that John talked about in these verses is Satan. In the verses where John talks about 'Egypt' and 'Sodom,' he was seeing things that happened during the French Revolution. Remember in the story of Moses, how the Egyptian pharaoh scornfully asked Moses, 'Who is this God that I should obey Him?' "

France Turns Away From God

"Yes," said Michael.

"Well, just like Pharaoh, France declared that it didn't believe in God either. So John was seeing the atheism of France when he talked about the sins of Pharaoh in Egypt."

"Does atheism mean not believing in God at all?"

"That's right," said Mother. "Some people know there is a God but don't trust Him or obey Him. An atheist does not even believe there is a God."

"So Egypt and Sodom and France were all atheist?"

"Yes," agreed Mother. "Sodom was known for its total lack of interest in anything that God told the people to do. Instead, the people in Sodom spent their time pursuing pleasure of the worst kind. The French people did this too. They treated marriage as if it meant nothing. According to Sir Walter Scott, France was the only nation in the world to openly lift her hand in rebellion against the Author of the universe. The French legislative assembly decreed that there was no God."

"Wow!" Michael said. "It would be pretty scary to stand up to God like that."

"France had a long history of defying God," Mother answered. "In 1572, the Saint Bartholomew's Day Massacre swept through France. Seventy thousand of God's people were murdered. In Paris, this massacre lasted for seven days; the first three were the worst. But throughout France, faithful Christians were being killed for as long as two months. The Catholic Church celebrated the slaughter, along with the pope and the king. A special medal was even made to honor the event, and an artist, named Vasari, painted three pictures about it that can still be seen in Rome today. They show men plotting with the French king, Charles IX, and then actually committing the massacres."

"You mean they not only killed all those people, but they were proud they had done it?" Michael exclaimed.

Mother nodded. "At the Adventist Church headquarters in Maryland, the Ellen G. White Estate has one of those medals."

"Can we go see it?" asked Michael.

"Yes, they keep it in a safe place. I'm sure they would be happy to show it to us."

"They probably keep it in the vault," guessed Michael. "They wouldn't want to lose something that interesting. Don't you think that it would be a good idea to go see it tomorrow instead of going to school?" He looked at his mother.

She smiled. "Nice try! Next time we visit the General Conference office will be soon enough.

"After the massacre, things got worse. In the past, France had helped the church keep God's Word away from the people; now the people of France turned away from the church and God Himself. The French assembly declared Christ an imposter and even put up a banner that said, 'Crush the Wretch,' meaning Christ. Bibles were burned, baptism and Communion were prohibited. Announcements were posted over burial places calling death an eternal sleep and denying the possibility of a resurrection.

"One French leader stood up in the General Assembly and shouted, 'God, if you exist, avenge Your injured name. I bid You defiance. You remain silent. You dare not launch Your thunder. Who after this will believe in Your existence?' "

"He actually challenged God out loud?" Michael asked.

Mother nodded. "The French people chose to worship the Goddess of Reason instead of the God of the universe. They took a young lady, not known for her spiritual qualities . . ."

"You mean a lady with a bad reputation?" interrupted Michael.

". . . and dressed her up to represent the Goddess of Reason," Mom continued, "and took her to the Notre Dame Cathedral where they worshiped her. 'This is our god,' they said."

"They broke the first commandment," observed Michael.

"Louis XV, who had been the king just before this time, realized that this terrible revolution was coming, yet he did nothing to prevent it. He didn't try to change any of the abuses by the aristocracy or by the church."

"The aristocracy was those people with all the power and money, wasn't it?" Michael wanted to know.

"That's right, but the aristocracy also included the relatives of the king. All of the terrible things that the church leaders and the nobles had done in the past to God's people were now done to the priests and the royal family and their relatives—even King Louis the XVI. This terrible time of blood and executions continued for three and a half years. Even today, it is referred to as the Reign of Terror."

"That must have been a terrible time," observed Michael, "even if the people who were being killed now were the ones who had been killing others before."

"Yes," agreed Mother, "it was a terrible time. But at the end of the three and a half years, France removed her declaration that there was no God. France tolerated the church and the Scriptures again. After this time the Bible was honored around the world as never before.

"In 1804, the British and Foreign Bible Society was started specifically to print the Bible in the common languages of the people and to spread it throughout the world. Today the Bible, or parts of it, have been printed in more than one thousand languages, and new languages are added every year."

"That's neat!" said Michael.

"Just as the prophet John foresaw, the Old Testament and the New Testament—the two witnesses who were killed—lay dead in the streets for three and a half years while the people celebrated. Then they came back to life. God could see the end from the beginning."

"He always does," said Michael, "doesn't He?"

"God is good to tell us ahead of time what's going to happen, so that even during those terrible dark times when people are dying and horrible things are happening, we know how things are going to end. We know Who will win in the end!" said Mother.

"Right!" agreed Michael.

16

Freedom in a New World

"Let's talk about a new country today," said Mother when she and Michael sat down to continue their discussion.

"What country is that?" asked Michael.

"One you are very familiar with," answered Mother. "In the 1500s England broke with the Catholic Church when King Henry VIII chose to separate and start the Church of England. But the Roman Church and the Church of England were very much alike. Some Christians in England wanted to practice their religion with the purity and simplicity of the early Christian church."

"But England isn't a new country," protested Michael. "We've talked about England before."

"I know," replied Mother. "But we have to talk about England to get to the part about the new country."

"Oh," said Michael.

"The Church of England had some traditions that it had gotten from the Roman Church even though there wasn't anything in the Bible about them. But since the Church of England was the only legal church in the country, people were not allowed to worship any other way. Some Christians just couldn't follow everything in the Church of England. They determined to worship and live as the Bible taught. They were called Puritans. They had to leave their homes and jobs and move to Holland. In England they had been farmers, but when they went to Holland, they had to learn to work with machines."

"That must have been hard," said Michael.

"God was preparing them for what would happen next," said Mother.

"Oh, I know what happened!" exclaimed Michael. "They went to America! America is the new country you said we were going to talk about, isn't it?"

"You're right," agreed Mother. "You see, if life had been easier for the Puritans in England, then they never would have gotten restless enough to search for a new place to live in the New World!

"They decided to go to the New World where they could find a land of their own among the English possessions. They wanted to be able to teach their children as they saw fit and to be able to worship as they felt the Bible said they should. They wanted religious freedom. They ended up in what we know today as Massachusetts.

"However, they didn't really understand what freedom means. They wanted freedom for themselves, but they were so sure they were right that they didn't give freedom to people who disagreed with them! The Puritans not only controlled the church, but they ran the government of the new colony as well. Any time a government forms an official religion, there will be trouble. So even in the new colony there was no real freedom. Only church members could say what should be done. Only church members had a voice in civil government."

"That wasn't fair!" exclaimed Michael.

"Everyone was required to contribute money to support the church and its leaders. Church attendance was required. Anyone skipping church was made to pay fines or go to prison or sometimes both.

"Not all the people were pleased about the way the Puritans made everyone follow their ideas. Roger Williams came from England to the colony eleven years after it was founded. He spoke out against the lack of religious freedom. 'Nobody should be forced to worship against his own will,' Mr. Williams said. But the leaders didn't change their rules. And Roger Williams didn't change his mind either. Finally, he was forced to leave the colony. He fled into the forests of the New World because of his stand against worship laws."

Michael wrinkled his forehead as he thought. "Why didn't the Puritans let people worship as they wanted to?" he asked. "After all, they had left England because people wouldn't let *them* worship the way they thought best."

"It wasn't easy for them to see all the truth at once," Mother replied. "The Reformation churches could see part of the truth, but they didn't go far enough. The Lutherans, for example, wouldn't go beyond what Luther had taught; the Calvinists stopped with what Calvin had taught them. But God still had many truths to reveal. It was like learning in school how to add and subtract but then refusing to go on and learn how to multiply and divide."

"Oh," said Michael. "I guess it would be hard to understand everything at once. But what happened to Roger Williams?"

"He spent months in the forest. He met an Indian tribe and lived with the Indians for some time. He established a small colony at Rhode Island. It was a safe place where people who had been oppressed because of their religious beliefs could go. There they really were allowed religious liberty."

"That's good!" said Michael.

"When the American Revolution came and the United States was established with a constitution, religious liberty actually became law," Mother continued. "The constitution reads, 'Congress shall make no law respecting an establishment of religion or prohibiting the free exercise thereof.' The news spread to Europe where many Christians excitedly received it. Was it true? Could there really be a place where a person could worship God in the way he wanted, instead of the way the government said he must? Many people flocked to the New World to escape tradition and religious oppression."

"What does 'tradition' mean?" Michael asked.

"Tradition means doing things a certain way, just because that is the way we've always done them. Tradition has always been a problem," Mother said. "It was a problem with the Jews when Jesus came. Rather than listen to what God said, they wanted to do things the way they always had. Later the Roman Church tried to make people do things its way, instead of learning from the Bible what God wanted them to do. As we've seen, even in the early colonial days of the United States, Protestants still had that problem."

Mom looked sober. "Tradition can still be a problem today. We should be willing to accept everything that God reveals to us from His Word. We need to let Him teach us what He wants us to know and not just insist on doing things the way we and other people always have."

"Yes," said Michael, "That must be what the Bible means when it says 'We ought to obey God rather than humans.' "

17

Signs of Jesus' Coming

"God has given us many promises of Jesus' second coming. Some of them were even given before Jesus had come the first time. Remember Enoch in the Old Testament?" Mother looked at Michael.

"Yes," he said. "Enoch was the man who lived longer than anyone else ever, ever, ever has!"

Mother laughed. "I guess that's right," she said. "We usually think of Enoch's son, Methuselah, as the person who lived the longest. But since Enoch never died and is still alive, I suppose that would make him the oldest man who ever lived."

"That's what I said!" exclaimed Michael.

"Well, when Enoch was preaching, a long time before he was taken to live with God, he talked about Jesus' second coming. We find what he said in verses 14 and 15 of the book of Jude." Mother picked up her Bible and read:

Enoch, the seventh descendant from Adam, said this about these people: "Look, the Lord is coming with thousands and thousands of his holy angels. The Lord will judge every person. He is coming to judge everyone and to punish all who are against God. He will punish them for all the evil they have done against him. And he will punish the sinners who are against God. He will punish them for all the evil things they have said against him."

"Jesus Himself also told us that He was coming back," said Michael.

"That's right," said Mother. "He did. One of His most famous quotations is found in John 14:1-3."

"Oh, I know those verses by heart," said Michael, "let me say them:"

> Jesus said, "Don't let your hearts be troubled. Trust in God. And trust in me. There are many rooms in my Father's house. I would not tell you this if it were not true. I am going there to prepare a place for you. After I go and prepare a place for you, I will come back. Then I will take you to be with me so that you may be where I am."

"Paul talked about Jesus' coming too," said Mother. "In 1 Thessalonians 4:16 he says:"

> The Lord himself will come down from heaven. There will be a loud command with the voice of the archangel and with the trumpet call of God. And those who have died and were in Christ will rise first.

"Paul probably knew about the Second Coming because Jesus had already lived here by the time Paul was writing, and he knew what Jesus had said about coming back," Michael said.

"Paul did know what Jesus had said," Mother agreed, "but the

MICHAEL ASKS WHY

Holy Spirit told Paul even more details. Paul's description is especially comforting to those who have had someone they love die. Paul didn't want Christians to feel sad or worried about loved ones who had died, so he described exactly what would happen when Jesus comes."

"I remember when Grandma Jo died and the minister read those verses. It made me feel better," said Michael.

"Me too," said Mother, hugging Michael. "Isaiah talked about Jesus' return too."

"Isaiah?" said Michael. "I knew he talked about Jesus' first coming because we learned about that in our Christmas play at school."

"Yes," said Mom, "but Isaiah also talked about Jesus' second coming. Why don't you read Isaiah 51:3?"

Michael got his Bible and found the verse in Isaiah. He read:

So the Lord will comfort Jerusalem. He will show mercy to those who live in her ruins. He will change her deserts into a garden like Eden. He will make her empty lands like the garden of the Lord. People there will be very happy. They will give thanks and sing songs.

"Now try Isaiah 62:4, 5 and Isaiah 35:1, 2," Mother said.

Again, Michael read:

You will never again be called the People that God Left. Your land will never again be called the Land that God Destroyed. You will be called the People God Loves. Your land will be called the Bride of God. This is because the Lord loves you. And your land will belong to him as a bride belongs to her husband. As a young man marries a woman, so your children will marry your land. As a man is very happy about his new wife, so your God will be happy with you. . . . The desert and dry land will become happy. The desert will be glad and will produce flowers. Like a flower, it will have many blooms. It will show its happiness, as if it is shouting with joy. It will be beautiful like the forest of Lebanon. It will be as beautiful as the hill of Carmel and the Plain of Sharon. All people will see the glory of the Lord. They will see the splendor of our God.

Michael looked up. "Wow! That's pretty neat! I didn't know Isaiah knew all of that!"

"Who else talked about Jesus' coming again?" asked Mother.

"*Um. . . .*" Michael thought. "The guy that wrote Revelation."

"That's right," said Mother. "Do you remember which of the disciples wrote Revelation?"

"Was it John?" asked Michael.

"Yes," said Mother. "John was one of Jesus' best friends. John missed Jesus when He went back to heaven; he wanted to see Jesus again so badly! John told us a lot about Jesus' second coming. Read Revelation 22:20, Michael."

Michael read:

Jesus is the One who says that these things are true. Now he says, "Yes, I am coming soon."

"But Bible writers weren't the only ones who talked about Jesus coming again. Martin Luther was excited about His return. And Luther's friend Melanchthon talked about it too. So did the reformer in Scotland, John Knox."

"I guess all Jesus' friends would be excited to see Him again, wouldn't they?" said Michael.

"Yes," said Mother. "All of us who love Jesus will be delighted to see Him again. We'll be even more happy to go live with Him and not have to deal with all the sad things that happen here on our earth."

"But Jesus said a lot of scary things would happen before He came." Michael seemed worried.

"That's true," said Mother. "The Bible tells us very clearly that a lot of the signs that Jesus is coming soon could be scary for some people."

"Didn't Jesus talk about earthquakes and stuff?" asked Michael.

"Yes, in Matthew 24 He talked about earthquakes. Since then, there have been some very large earthquakes."

"I remember when there was an earthquake in Mexico," said Michael, "and one in California."

"One of the worst earthquakes that our earth has survived was in 1755," said Mother.

"That was a long time ago."

"Yes," said Mother, "but people were looking forward to Jesus' second coming back then too, and they recognized this earthquake as a sign that the earth was getting older and that we didn't have as long to wait until Jesus came."

"Tell me about it," said Michael. "Where did it hit?"

"The worst part of the earthquake was in Lisbon."

"That's in Portugal. I learned that in geography," said Michael. "We learned about earthquakes too. The worst spot in an earthquake is called the epicenter."

"Well, the epicenter of this earthquake was in Lisbon, Portugal. But it shook many countries in Europe and Africa. It was even felt in America, Greenland, and the West Indies. In fact," said Mother, "the earth shook so hard that the quake could be felt for over four million square miles. In Cadiz, Spain, there was a tidal wave, following the earthquake, that was sixty feet tall."

"Sixty feet!" said Michael. "Are tidal waves that big?"

"Not usually," said Mother. "And even worse, during the earthquake the water ran a long way out into the ocean, leaving a lot of land that was usually covered by water. People rushed down to the harbor to see what was going on, and when the tidal wave rolled back in, they were all drowned."

Signs of Jesus' Coming

"That sounds terrible," said Michael.

"Historians have estimated that about ninety thousand people died," said Mother. "Jesus predicted other signs besides earthquakes to let us know that He was coming again."

"Didn't He say that the sun would become dark and the moon would, too, and that the stars would fall out of the sky? That sounds impossible," Michael said.

"It probably sounded pretty impossible to the people who were listening to Jesus, because they had never seen anything like that happen before. But it happened."

"Really?" said Michael. "When?"

"On May 19, 1780, twenty-five years after the Lisbon earthquake, the sun and moon were darkened, just like Jesus said."

"What happened?" asked Michael.

"It started out like a normal sunny day," replied Mother. "Farmers were doing their work, and their animals were out grazing in the fields. But in the late morning, clouds rolled in. It looked like maybe there would be a thunderstorm. There wasn't much rain, but the sky just kept getting darker and darker. Even the cows knew something was wrong. They all walked back to the barns, thinking it was evening and time to be milked. The sky got darker and still darker."

"What about the people?" asked Michael. "Did they understand what was going on?"

"No," said Mother. "Many of them were afraid and thought it was the end of the world."

"But it wasn't," said Michael, "because we're still here."

"That's true," said Mother. "But people remembered that Jesus had said these things would happen before He came again, and it made them study their Bibles."

"Then it was a good thing," said Michael.

"Yes," said Mother, "it was a good thing. That same evening another strange thing happened. When the moon came up, it was a dark red color. It was so dark that it didn't give any light. It was a very dark night, and many people were afraid of that too."

"But the Bible said that was going to happen," said Michael. "It was in the same verse about the sun."

"Well, the people who had studied their Bibles weren't afraid; they were excited. They knew it meant that things were happening just as Jesus said they would."

"What about the stars?" said Michael.

"That comes later," said Mother. "You remember that Jesus also said there would be a lot of bad people and a lot of bad things happening in the world just before He returns. He said it would be just like it was in the days of Noah."

"In the days of Noah, things were so bad that God had to destroy the earth," Michael said.

"Things will be very bad again before Jesus comes," Mother said. "There will be a lot of people who don't love Jesus and who don't care about His feelings and who don't keep His laws."

"It sounds like lots of people will get hurt then," said Michael. "That's what happened in Noah's day. The Flood came."

"Yes," said Mother, "whenever people disregard God's laws, people get hurt."

"But, how come it has to be like that? The Bible tells us exactly what's going to happen. People know He's going to come."

Mother put her arms around Michael. "That's true, but do you remember the story about Baby Jesus coming to Bethlehem? People were looking for Jesus to come then too. But only a few people were really prepared to see Him. Not many noticed when He did actually come. It will be like that before Jesus comes the second time. We know He's coming because He told us in the Bible. And we know the things that will happen before He comes. But many people are not getting ready to meet Him."

"That must make Him really sad."

"Yes, I think it does," said Mother.

"Well, I'll be happy to see Him," said Michael.

"And He'll be happy to see you too," Mother answered.

18

William Miller's Prediction

When Michael and Mother next sat down to continue the story of how God had helped men and women to know about His truth and follow Him, Mother said, "Have you ever heard of a man named William Miller?"

"I think so," Michael answered. "Who was he?"

"William Miller was a farmer in the northeastern United States. He had been a Christian when he was younger, but after a while he became a deist."

"What's a deist?" asked Michael.

"A deist is someone who believes in God and believes that God created the world, but does not believe that God has anything to do with the earth anymore. They think He just sort of got everything going and then left the world to run itself."

"That would be depressing," said Michael.

"Well," said Mother, "it was depressing to William Miller too. He was very discouraged because he felt sinful. Finally, the Holy Spirit led him to believe that Jesus really did come to save people.

MICHAEL ASKS WHY

So William Miller got out his Bible and started studying. He wanted to learn more about Jesus. The more he studied, the more beautiful Jesus became to him. The more he studied, the more interested he became, and he found that Daniel and Revelation were his favorite books in the Bible. As he looked at the different signs of Jesus' coming, he realized that many of them had already been fulfilled."

"Like the Dark Day and the earthquakes we talked about yesterday?" Michael asked.

"Yes. William Miller noticed that these things had been predicted in the Bible. At that time, some Christians thought the promises about Jesus coming again just meant that He would come into a person's heart and that He really didn't mean that He would actually come back to earth. Others thought there would be a thousand years of peace before Jesus came. During this thousand years, everyone would learn to be happy and love each other; they would accept Jesus into their hearts and worship Him. Then Jesus would come."

"A thousand years is an awfully long time to wait for something," Michael said. "I'm glad we know Jesus is really coming and that He is coming soon."

"Well, we owe a lot to William Miller for studying the Bible for himself with the help of the Holy Spirit. When he began to study the Bible, he decided to just start reading in Genesis and keep reading until he came to something he didn't understand. Then he would stop and use a concordance . . . "

"A concord . . . a what?" Michael asked.

"A concordance," Mother answered. "It's a large book that lists all the words in the Bible and where you can find them in the Bible—in which texts. When Miller came to something he didn't understand, he would look up all the other texts in the Bible that talked about the subject. Then he would read all these texts until he felt he understood. Then he would go on. He liked to study for himself."

William Miller's Prediction

"I'm kind of like that," said Michael. I want to study for myself instead of just listening to what other people say."

"William Miller was like you in another way too. He liked math, just like you do."

"Did he?" asked Michael. "How do you know?"

"Because when he came to the book of Daniel and read about the prophecy of the 2,300 days, he started doing some figuring."

"What prophecy is that?" asked Michael.

"Daniel said that after 2,300 days the sanctuary would be cleansed. Miller believed the earth was the sanctuary and that it would be cleansed by fire when Jesus came the second time. So he thought that if he could figure out when the 2,300 days started, he would know when Jesus would come. William Miller looked and looked, but he couldn't tell when the starting point of the 2,300 days should be.

"Then he found another prophecy in Daniel that talked about seventy weeks that would begin with the decree to rebuild Jerusalem. As he studied more, William Miller found that the two prophecies had the same beginning point. He knew from history that the Persian king, Artaxerxes, issued a decree in 457 B.C. to rebuild Jerusalem. Remember that earlier we said in Bible prophecy a day often equals a year in real time?"

"Yes," Michael said.

"William Miller knew that seventy weeks times seven days in each week equals 490 days, or years. So he counted 490 years from 457 B.C. and came to the year A.D. 34. What happened in A.D. 34?"

"*Um,* well . . ." said Michael, "Jesus was 34 years old!"

"Actually," Mother laughed, "He wasn't. Historians had a little trouble figuring out the year when Jesus was born. Later they realized that they were about three or four years off. So Jesus was probably born in the year 3 or 4 B.C."

"Oh," said Michael, "then Jesus would have been about thirty-seven years old in A.D. 34."

```
┌──── "Seventy weeks (490 years) are determined upon thy people" ────
├──── 7 weeks ──────────── 62 weeks ──────────── 1 week ────
│
│ 457 B.C.              408 B.C.                  27 A.D.
│ The decree to rebuild  Restoration of Jerusalem  Baptism of
│ Jerusalem             completed                 Jesus Christ
```

The 2300 Days (Years) of Amazing Bible Prophecy

"Except," said Mother "that Jesus was back in heaven by A.D. 34. Let's do some math and figure this out."

"Tell me the numbers," said Michael, "I have my pencil and paper here now."

"In Daniel 9:24-27 the angel explains that the seventy weeks are divided into sections as you see in this picture chart. But let's do the math for ourselves," said Mother. "From the time of Artaxerxes' decree to rebuild Jerusalem it was seven 'weeks' until Jerusalem was completely restored."

"Seven weeks," repeated Michael. "That would mean seven times seven or forty-nine years. Now I need to subtract forty-nine from 457. That's 408."

"OK," said Mom. "That brings us to 408 B.C. Then, it was another sixty-two weeks from the complete restoration of Jerusalem until Jesus was baptized."

"Hold on!" Michael said, "Sixty-two times seven would be . . . OK, that would be 434 years."

"Now subtract 408 from 434 and see what you get."

After some figuring, Michael announced, "That equals twenty-six. What would that mean?"

"According to Daniel's prophecy, that would be when Jesus, the Messiah, would begin His work," Mother said. "But there is something else. Do you understand about B.C. and A.D.?"

"Sure, that means 'Before Christ' and 'After Death.'"

William Miller's Prediction

	1810 years to the sanctuary cleansing	
31 A.D. Crucifixion of Jesus Christ	34 A.D. Stoning of Stephen	1844 A.D. Cleansing of the Sanctuary

"Actually A.D. stands for *Anno Domini* which, in Latin, means 'Year of our Lord.' But," persisted Mom, "do you understand how the change from B.C. to A.D. would look on a time line?"

"What do you mean?" asked Michael.

"Well, think about the years before Jesus was born as counting down to His birth—four, three, two one—just like the countdown to a rocket launch. Then we count the years after Jesus was born as going up—one, two, three, four. Of course, the people who lived then didn't think of it that way."

Michael looked puzzled. "So you mean Mary and Joseph and their neighbors didn't know the way of counting years was changing?"

"Oh no," said Mother. "It wasn't until hundreds of years later that people started separating time into the years before Christ was born and the years afterward. But let's finish our math now. When the B.C. years count down to 1, they stop. Then the A.D. years begin counting up with 1. So you have 2 years that are named 1. The B.C. 1 and the A.D. 1. There is no year called 0. So when you subtract 408 years from 434 B.C., you are crossing over into A.D. years. That means you have to add one because there were two different years named 1."

"I think I understand," said Michael.

"Then, what number do you have now?" asked Mother.

"A.D. 27. What happened then?"

"That was the year Jesus was baptized," replied Mother. "Just like the prophecy in Daniel said, it was 408 years from the restoration of Jerusalem until Jesus began His work as the Messiah. Now we need to add the last week of the seventy-week prophecy. The prophecy said that the seventy weeks were for the Jews. So we have the forty-nine years of restoring Jerusalem, then 434 years to Jesus' baptism, and finally seven more years for the gospel to be preached especially to the Jews. If you add seven more years to A.D. 27, what do you have?"

"That would be A.D. 34," said Michael.

"And that is when Stephen was stoned and the gospel began to go to all the world, not just to the Jews," Mother said.

"OK," said Michael. "So if we add forty-nine years plus 434 years plus seven years, we get 490 years. And that's exactly what seventy weeks would be if each day equaled an actual year! Wow. The prophecy really works out mathematically, doesn't it?"

"But remember that William Miller was trying to find out when the 2,300 days, or years, ended. He read in Daniel that the seventy weeks were part of the 2,300 days, and he found that both periods began at the same time. So if the seventy weeks and the 2,300 days both began at the same time and the seventy weeks ended in A.D. 34, how could William Miller find out when the 2,300 days ended?"

"He would have to subtract 490 years, the seventy weeks, from 2,300 years," Michael replied, "to find out how many more years the 2,300 years lasted. Let's see . . . 2,300 minus 490 equals 1,810."

"That's right," said Mother. "But we learned that the seventy weeks ended in A.D. 34. So you have to add the 1,810 years and A.D. 34 to find the year that the 2,300-day prophecy ended."

"That would be 1844," Michael said.

"That's the answer William Miller came up with too," said Mother. "By doing all the same math that you've done, he figured out that the sanctuary would be cleansed, according to Daniel's prophecy, sometime around 1844, although he wasn't sure exactly when. William Miller was convinced that the 'sanctuary' meant the

William Miller's Prediction

'world' and that it would be cleansed with fire when Jesus returned and created a new world with no sin. He realized there weren't very many years left until 1844. As the time came closer, he gave up farming and started preaching. He wanted to let everyone know right away that Jesus was coming very soon.

"In nearly every town there were dozens or even hundreds of people who accepted Miller's teachings. Protestant churches everywhere let Mr. Miller preach, and thousands of people decided to get ready for Jesus' soon coming. Many people did not agree with his math, but they did believe that Jesus was coming soon."

"No wonder some people didn't agree with his math," said Michael. "It's pretty hard to figure it all out. What religion was William Miller?"

"William Miller was a Baptist," said Mother, "and many Baptists supported him.

"In 1833, two years after William Miller started preaching about Jesus' soon coming, there was a big meteor shower," continued Mother.

"I've seen a meteor," said Michael.

"Yes," said Mother. "Sometimes we see falling stars, and sometimes there are meteor showers when we see several falling stars at once. Astronomers can predict when most of these are going to happen; we can even look up in the almanac the time when we're most likely to see falling stars. But this event was different. It went on for hours and hours. People were afraid that all of the stars were falling out of the sky and that there wouldn't be any left."

"So everything happened just like Jesus said it would," Michael said.

"Revelation 6:13 describes it like this: 'The stars of heaven fell to the earth like figs falling from a fig tree when the wind blows.' And it happened just like the Bible said. This made even more people believe William Miller's message and get ready for Jesus' soon coming.

"The press and the newspapers made fun of Mr. Miller. They

made him sound like a crazy man who had left his home to travel all over the place preaching strange ideas. They called him a fanatic and a liar. They made fun of the people who believed him and said they were crazy too."

"But Mom," said Michael, "William Miller was wrong; Jesus didn't come in 1844. Does that mean that he wasn't really one of God's people?"

"No," said Mother. "William Miller loved God very much. He did not understand what the prophecy was talking about when it said that the sanctuary would be cleansed. His math wasn't wrong, but he was wrong about what would happen when the 2,300 days were finished. But he did get thousands of people to think seriously about Jesus' soon coming. And he did get people to start reading their Bibles and to prepare their hearts to meet Jesus. And that was important."

"But if William Miller's math was right, what really did happen in 1844?" Michael wanted to know.

"We'll talk about that next time," Mother assured him.

19

The Great Disappointment

"Mom," said Michael, "Jesus didn't come in 1844. What about all those people who were expecting Him?"

"They were very disappointed," said Mother. "Often humans have trouble understanding God and His plans. But somehow God's true message still gets out even though people make mistakes in trying to interpret what God really means. Although William Miller was wrong about the *time* when Jesus was going to come and even though he was wrong about what the cleansing of the sanctuary meant, he was right that Jesus was going to come back to earth, and people needed to hear that message. All through time people have had trouble understanding what God means because human tradition has gotten in the way. The things that people expect to happen are not necessarily what God has in mind. This happened to the first disciples too."

"I know," said Michael. "They expected Jesus to be a king and overthrow the Romans. Instead, He died. That must have been a great disappointment too."

"It was," said Mother. "Their mistake and disappointment was a lot like William Miller's mistake and disappointment. William Miller was mistaken because he accepted the popular view of the sanctuary. At that time, most Christians thought the sanctuary was the earth. Jesus' disciples were mistaken because they accepted the popular view of the Messiah as a king.

"Miller and his followers could have understood better what the prophecy was talking about if they had studied the sanctuary Moses and the Israelites built. They would have learned that, for the High Priest working in the sanctuary, the very last duty of the year was to cleanse it. This service was called the Day of Atonement, and it symbolized the removal of sin from Israel. The sanctuary that Moses built in the wilderness was a copy of the one in heaven, so when Jesus went to cleanse the sanctuary in heaven, it meant that He was going to deal with the sins of His people like the High Priest in the Old Testament did once a year for Israel. So when the prophecy in Daniel talks about cleansing the sanctuary, it is talking about a similar work that takes place in the sanctuary in heaven, and it is called the judgment."

"Judgment?" asked Michael.

"Yes. During the service of the Day of Atonement in Moses' time, there was a whole week of investigation. The people searched their hearts and confessed all their sins. In heaven, the judgment is when Jesus goes through the records of each person and looks at how they have searched their hearts and confessed their sins."

"Then William Miller was wrong about Jesus coming back. He made a mistake; his whole message was for nothing," said Michael.

"No, that's not true," said Mother. "God wanted William Miller to tell people that the 2,300 days in Daniel's prophecy had come to an end and that the signs of Jesus' coming had been fulfilled. It was time to get ready to meet Him. Just like the disciples were mistaken in what they expected the Messiah to do at the end of the seventy weeks, so Adventists were mistaken in what they expected

The Great Disappointment

God to do at the end of the 2,300 days. They didn't completely understand the prophecies, yet God's work still was done just the way He wanted. God wanted people to realize He was coming soon. He wanted them to get ready to meet Him."

"So, William Miller was a good guy after all?" asked Michael.

"Yes," said Mother, "he was."

"But what happened to the people who believed William Miller and followed him?"

"When Jesus didn't come, they were terribly disappointed. Some of them turned away from God completely. Some of them went back to the churches they had belonged to before they left to follow William Miller. The rest divided into two groups. One group became the Advent Christian Church, and one became the Seventh-day Adventist Church."

"Was William Miller an Adventist, then?" Michael asked.

"William Miller never became a Seventh-day Adventist," said Mother. "But anyone who is eagerly waiting for Jesus to come the second time is a real 'Adventist' because that word means someone who is looking forward to Jesus' coming."

20

Looking for Jesus

"Michael," said Mother when they sat down to talk the next evening, "why don't you read Revelation 14:6, 7 in your Bible?"

"OK," said Michael, picking up his Bible and turning the pages. "Here it is."

> Then I saw another angel flying high in the air. The angel had the eternal Good News to preach to those who live on earth—to every nation, tribe, language, and people. The angel said in a loud voice, "Fear God and give Him praise. The time has come for God to judge all people. Worship God. He made the heavens, the earth, the sea, and the springs of water."

"Thank you," said Mother. "When the angel said 'every nation, tribe, language, and people,' the angel meant that preaching the Good News would be a worldwide movement. For many years, the message about Jesus had been preached in parts of Europe, northern Africa, and Asia, but now it was time for the message about Jesus' second coming to spread to the rest of the world.

"In Germany, there was a Jewish boy named Joseph Wolff. His dad was a rabbi, and he had been taught to be a very good Jew. When he asked his dad 'Who was Jesus?' his dad told him that Jesus was a very talented Jew, but he had been executed for pretending to be the Messiah.

" 'Oh,' said Joseph. 'But why is Jerusalem destroyed, and why are the Jews in captivity now?'

" 'It's very sad,' said Joseph's dad, 'but over and over again, the Jews have murdered the prophets God sent to us, and now our city is destroyed and our country is overrun by other people.'

"Joseph got to thinking. *What if Jesus was innocent? What if he really was the Messiah just like He said He was? What if, what if?* he kept thinking.

"When Joseph was seven years old, he was talking to an elderly Christian man who lived nearby. 'Someday the Messiah is going to come,' Joseph bragged, 'and then Jerusalem will be the capitol of the whole world, and everybody will respect us Jews!'

"The old man smiled and said, 'Joseph, let me tell you about the Messiah.' He explained about Jesus and His humble life and how He died.

" 'But, the Messiah was supposed to be a king!' young Joseph blurted out.

" 'Yes,' said the old man, 'but read what the prophets really said. Go home and read Isaiah 53.' As Joseph read the chapter, he was convinced that Jesus Christ was the Son of God. The Scriptures talked about Jesus being a suffering servant, about going like a sheep to the slaughter. *Could there be two comings of the Messiah?* Joseph wondered. *Could He have come one time as a suffering servant, and was He going to come again as a victorious king?* It certainly fit with the things that Jesus said about Himself.

"When Joseph was eleven years old, he left home to get an education. He lived with relatives near where he was going to school. However, the more he studied and the more he talked about what he was studying, the more angry his family became. Eventually he was thrown out for talking about his Christian beliefs. Joseph decided if he was going to be a Christian, he needed to join the Christian church. So he became a Catholic. He attended a Catholic college in Rome. However, he saw that the church was not operating as it should in caring for people. It seemed more interested in getting their money than in helping them spiritually. Joseph Wolff began to attack these abuses in the church zealously.

"The leaders of the church called him a heretic, and Joseph had to leave the school. He went to England and studied there for two years. While he was studying, he became a Protestant and was convinced that Jesus was coming soon. He read the prophecies of Daniel and worked on the same mathematical problems as William Miller. And he came up with an answer only a few years different from the one William Miller had predicted. If Jesus was coming that soon, Joseph decided, then he needed to tell people quickly.

"Joseph traveled to Africa, preaching in Egypt and Ethiopia. Then he went to Asia and preached in Palestine, Syria, Persia, Bokhara, and India. Later Dr. Wolff (Joseph had a doctoral degree by then), visited the United States. He preached in New York, Philadelphia, Baltimore, and Washington, D.C. During Dr. Wolff's many missionary journeys, Satan tried hard to make him stop preaching. Through the years, in various places, he was sold as a slave, starved, put in prison, condemned to death three times, robbed, and one time stripped of everything he owned and made to hike over a mountain barefoot in the snow! Yet, God was with Joseph, and he never gave up. Until he died, he continued preaching about Jesus' soon coming."

"He had a really exciting life," interjected Michael.

"When we are following the plans God has for us, life can be exciting," Mom said.

"Dr. Wolff wasn't the only one to spread the message about Jesus' soon coming. In South America, a Spanish priest named

Looking for Jesus

Lacunza studied the Bible and also found that Jesus was returning soon. As a Catholic priest, he knew that he could be killed for his beliefs, so he wrote books under the name of Rabbi Ben Ezra, pretending he was a converted Jew. In 1825, his book about Jesus' soon coming reached London and led many English people to give their hearts to Jesus.

"In Germany about the same time, a Lutheran minister named Bengel was also studying the Bible carefully. He, too, did the math in Daniel's prophecies and realized that Jesus must be coming soon. His mathematical calculations agreed quite closely with William Miller's. Members of his church took his message to the people in Russia.

"Meanwhile, God had someone in Switzerland as well. In Geneva, a man named Gaussen became convinced that Jesus was coming soon. Gaussen began by teaching the children. He wrote books for them in French explaining about Jesus' soon coming. Later when he preached to adults and they told him that 'Daniel and Revelation are just too hard for us to understand,' Gaussen laughed and said, 'They can't be that hard to understand. Ask your children; they'll explain them to you.' And the children did!

"Switzerland wasn't the only place where children were telling adults about the good news of Jesus' coming. In Scandinavia preachers were preaching about Jesus' soon coming, but the leaders of the country put them in prison. Children six, seven, and eight years old then preached the message and spread the news of Jesus' soon coming all over Scandinavia in a way that adults never could have done!

"All over the world people were asking 'What must I do to be saved?' Isolated Christian groups in many different countries were discovering, just from studying their Bibles, that Jesus was coming soon. The Holy Spirit was leading them all to the same conclusion."

"But Mom," said Michael, "Jesus didn't come in the 1840s, no matter what date they figured out."

"That's right," said Mother. "Jesus said in Matthew 24:36, 'No one knows when that day or time will be. Even the Son and the angels in heaven don't know. Only the Father knows.' But we are told that we can know when it is near. We can do this by studying Bible prophecy. So even though these people were confused about what was actually going to happen in the 1840's, they spread the good news of Jesus all over the world."

"So it was a good thing anyway, even though they didn't understand?" asked Michael.

"Yes it was," said Mother. "No one who experienced the waiting for Jesus in 1844 could ever forget it. If only God's people still had the same searching hearts today! We need to pray and study like they did then."

21

Losing
Faith

"When William Miller first started preaching, the leaders of the churches were not sure how to respond to him," Mother told Michael the next evening. "However, as they saw more and more people flooding into their churches, they decided to support him. Later, when they realized that all of these new members wanted *them* to preach about Jesus' second coming too, they rejected William Miller and his message. Then the pastors told their members not to go to his meetings anymore.

"A strange thing happened. After the leaders of the different churches rejected William Miller, interest in church attendance seemed to drop. In a short time, over fifty thousand Christians withdrew from the churches they had been attending and started meeting together with others who were looking for Jesus to come back soon. Until this time, most of those who believed Miller's message had remained in their own churches. But now there was a huge exodus. Ministers noticed that conversions were few and far between."

"You can't blame the people for leaving, if their churches

weren't interested in Jesus coming back," said Michael. "What kind of church would that be?"

"That's right," Mother agreed. "The Bible talks about this kind of problem. It's called having a form of religion, but lacking godliness. But among the thousands of Christians who left their churches to follow William Miller, the very opposite was taking place. They were spending even more time studying their Bibles and praying. Ellen White wrote: 'If God's professed people would receive the light as it shines upon them from His word, they would reach that unity for which Christ prayed, that which the apostle describes, "the unity of the Spirit in the bond of peace" ' (*The Great Controversy,* 379).That's exactly what was happening among the 'Millerites,' as William Miller's followers became known. Their message was called the 'Advent' message because the word *advent* means 'coming' and they talked so much about the coming of Jesus."

"Is that why our church is called the Adventist Church?" Michael asked. "Because we believe Jesus is coming soon?"

"Yes," Mother answered. "Now, Michael, would you please read Ephesians 4:3-5?"

"Sure," said Michael. He found the place in his Bible, and began to read:

> You are joined together with peace through the Spirit. Do all you can to continue together in this way. Let peace hold you together. There is one body and one Spirit. And God called you to have one hope. There is one Lord, one faith, and one baptism.

"Thank you," said Mother. "Among the Millerites, denominational barriers broke down, and they became one. Drawn from all the well-known churches of that day, those who had accepted the advent message were able to worship together in unity as they anxiously awaited Jesus' coming. But, sadly, most churches rejected the message that Jesus was coming soon.

Losing Faith

"Revelation 14:8 says: 'Then the second angel followed the first angel and said, "She [Babylon] is destroyed! . . . She made all the nations drink the wine of her adultery and of God's anger." ' In Revelation 17, the Bible refers to the church as a pure, clean woman, and it refers to Babylon as an adulterous woman whose clothes were red from the blood of the martyrs. All the way through the Old Testament, God talks about being married to His church, or His people. When His church is unfaithful to Him, God calls it adultery. When Revelation talks of the daughters of the adulterous woman, it is talking about churches that cling to false doctrines and traditions instead of taking all of their beliefs, straight and pure, from the Bible.

"Leaders in churches that rejected the advent message turned people away from the truth. In Revelation 18:4 John says: 'Then I heard another voice from heaven say: "Come out of that city, my people, so that you will not share in her sins. Then you will not receive the terrible things that will happen to her." ' "

"Is that what the Millerites were doing—coming out of those churches that weren't interested in Jesus' coming?" asked Michael. "Does that mean that people who attend those churches today are not good Christians?"

"Not at all," said Mother. "There are many people who love God in all churches."

"But if they love God, why aren't they doing what He has asked them to do? Isn't that how we show God we love Him—by obeying Him?"

"Some Christians don't understand that God still wants us to keep all of His commandments. But we can be sure that before the judgment is over, every individual will have a chance to choose to do things God's way," Mother said seriously.

"But how can we tell which people belong to God and which don't?" persisted Michael.

"We can't," replied Mother. "And anyway, that's not our job. Jesus is the only fair judge because only He knows what people are thinking and the reasons why they do what they do."

"Well, I'm glad Jesus is my only judge," Michael said, "since He understands me and is my best Friend."

22

Looking for Answers

"Michael," said Mother, "let's look up the story of the ten virgins in Matthew 25."

"Oh, I know that story," said Michael. "They were all waiting for a wedding with little oil lamps, but they had to wait too long for the groom to come, and all ten virgins fell asleep. When they woke up, he was coming, but five of them didn't have any oil left for their lamps. They had to run to town quickly to buy some more. The other five had brought extra oil. They were able to go into the wedding with him."

"Very good, Michael! This story describes the early Adventists, the followers of William Miller who were looking forward to Jesus' coming. They knew that Jesus was coming. All of the signs Jesus had talked about had taken place—the destruction of Jerusalem, the persecution of the church during the Dark Ages, the sun being darkened, the moon not giving light, and the stars falling from heaven. All of the people who believed in the advent message were excited about Jesus' coming, just like all ten virgins were excited about the bridegroom's coming.

"The oil in that story represented the Holy Spirit. Some bridesmaids didn't have extra oil with them. They had joined the wedding party on impulse, not prepared for trials or delay. When the time came for the groom to come, their lamps were out of oil. The disappointment in 1844 was bitter, and many of the believers couldn't handle the delay and the embarrassment when Jesus didn't come. Some had joined the Millerites out of fear, or they had depended on the faith of others rather than studying God's Word for themselves, so they did not have the Holy Spirit to help them through the trials.

"During this time, there were many fanatics who went way beyond the bounds of common sense. These fanatics gave the rest of the Adventist group a bad reputation, and most of the Adventist believers had no sympathy with these people. Satan is the accuser of the brethren. He always watches carefully for errors and defects among God's people and then points them out so everybody notices, while many good things they do go entirely unmentioned.

"In times of renewed faith, Satan brings in people who have ungodly hearts and unbalanced minds. They become the fanatics of the group. Fanatical Christians were a problem even in Luther's day."

"They're a problem now too," said Michael.

"Yes," said Mother, "they are. It's one of Satan's ways of interfering with God's message. But we shouldn't give up on God's church just because it includes some fanatics.

"All the Millerites were expecting Jesus to come in the autumn of 1844. Some farmers who were expecting His coming left their crops in the fields and the potatoes still in the ground. They spent time searching their hearts for any sins they should confess while waiting for Jesus to come.

"Of course, He didn't come, and the Millerites were bitterly disappointed. Many people gave up their faith. Ellen White tells us that their disappointment at that time was terrible, but it was not as great as the disappointment experienced by the disciples when Jesus died."

"That must have been even worse," Michael agreed.

"After 1844, people expected Adventism to disappear. After all, these people had been expecting Jesus to come, and He hadn't. However, God's people who had been searching their hearts and humbly reading His Word recognized that the Holy Spirit had really been working. There must be a different answer. There must have been a mistake. They remembered the story of Jonah."

"You mean, because Jonah told the people of Nineveh that the city was going to be destroyed and it didn't turn out that way?" said Michael. "Maybe there was something else that the 1844 people didn't understand."

"You're right," said Mother. "Looking back on the whole experience, William Miller said he would not have done anything differently. He had felt at the time that God wanted him to preach that message, and he did what God told him. God didn't abandon His people in their terrible disappointment. Even though they couldn't understand what His plan was, they trusted Him and stayed faithful to Him."

23

Cleaning God's Temple in Heaven

"Until the great disappointment in 1844, most Christians thought that the sanctuary mentioned in Daniel's prophecy referred to the earth. So, when William Miller read that the sanctuary would be cleansed at the end of 2,300 days, he thought the prophecy meant that the earth would be cleansed by fire at the second coming of Jesus. When Jesus didn't come and the world didn't end, the Millerites were very confused. Why didn't Jesus come? What was the mistake?"

"Was there a problem with William Miller's math?" asked Michael.

"No," said Mother, "his calculations were all correct. But he just didn't understand that the sanctuary was actually in heaven. Why don't you read Hebrews 9:1-5 and tell me what you think it says."

Michael read for a few minutes and then said, "It's talking about God's instructions for a place for worship. He said to set up a holy tent for worship. The first area in the tent was called the Holy Place.

Cleaning God's Temple in Heaven

In it were a lamp and a table with bread that was made especially for God. There was a golden altar for burning incense too. A curtain separated this part from the next room, which was called the Most Holy Place. The only thing in there was a wooden box called the ark that was covered with gold. Inside this box were the Ten Commandments, a golden jar of manna, and Aaron's rod that had once grown leaves and buds and almonds. On top of the ark were two angels made of gold whose wings met above the lid."

"Very good!" said Mother. "Now I'll read Hebrews 8:1, 2."

> Here is the point of what we are saying: We do have a high priest who sits on the right side of God's throne in heaven. Our high priest serves in the Most Holy Place. He serves in the true place of worship that was made by God, not by men.

"That doesn't sound like the sanctuary is the same thing as the earth," said Michael. "In fact, it sounds like the sanctuary is in heaven."

"That's right," said Mother. "The original sanctuary was in heaven. The sanctuary that Moses built in Old Testament times was a copy of the one in heaven. Three Bible writers tell us that there is a sanctuary in heaven: First, Moses says he built the one in the Old Testament after a pattern God showed him. Then Paul talks about the sanctuary in heaven and the fact that it was the pattern for the one Moses built on earth. And finally, John actually saw the sanctuary in heaven in a vision and described it in the book of Revelation.

"In order to understand what Jesus is doing now in the sanctuary in heaven, we need to understand what happened in the sanctuary that was on earth. Every day the priests offered sacrifices for the people. In addition, people could bring their own sin offerings. They would place their hands on the head of the animal and confess their sins. Then the animal would be killed, and the priest would take its blood into the Holy Place and sprinkle it before the curtain that separated the two rooms—the Holy Place and the Most Holy Place. This represented the fact that the sin had been forgiven and that it had been transferred to the sanctuary itself.

"Then, once a year, on the Day of Atonement, the priest chose two perfect goats. He cast lots over them—this was an old-fashioned way of drawing straws—to determine which one was the 'Lord's goat' and which one was the 'evil goat.' Then the priest sacrificed the Lord's goat and took the blood past the curtain into the Most Holy Place where he sprinkled it on the top of the ark. In this way, the priest, in symbol, gathered up all the sins of the Israelites for the past year and carried them out of the sanctuary.

"After leaving the sanctuary, the High Priest placed his hands on the head of the 'evil goat' and confessed all the sins of Israel. That represented transferring all the sins onto the goat. Then the goat was taken out into the wilderness and turned loose. It was called the 'scapegoat.' "

"Oh," said Michael. "I've heard of a scapegoat at school. That's what we call someone who gets punished for something someone else did."

"Yes," said Mother, "this is where that word came from. Now, as I was saying about the Day of Atonement, when the scapegoat was taken away, it took with it all the sins that had been held in the sanctuary all year."

"What about the sins of somebody who hadn't confessed?" interrupted Michael. "Would the scapegoat carry away those sins too?"

"No," said Mother. "It was really important to have all sins confessed and forgiven before the Day of Atonement, otherwise the person remained guilty until he or she confessed."

"I know how bad that feels!" exclaimed Michael.

"When Jesus went back to heaven, He took the job of being our High Priest and worked in the heavenly sanctuary. Like the earthly High Priest who took the confessed sins on himself, Jesus does that for His followers. When we confess our sins, we never need to worry about them again because Jesus takes them and forgives us.

"Daniel's prophecy says that the sanctuary was to be cleansed at the end of the 2,300 days. In Bible times, the sanctuary on earth was cleansed by the work of atonement. And so now the heavenly sanctuary would be cleansed that way too. In 1844, at the end of the 2,300-day prophecy, Jesus began working in the Most Holy Place of the sanctuary in heaven. He began carrying out the work that was symbolized on the Day of Atonement in the Old Testament— removing all the confessed sins over all the years.

"Everyone who repents of sin and has faith in Jesus is entitled to the benefits of His atonement. In order to show that God is just, the records are examined. We believe that in 1844 Jesus began the work of investigation, examining the records to determine who has had faith in Him and repented of sin."

"Hmm," said Michael, "He's been doing it a long time; He must be almost done."

"He must be," Mother agreed. "So it's important for us to be ready every day to meet Him."

24

What Is Jesus Doing Now?

"The early Adventists now understood that the cleansing of the sanctuary and Jesus' second coming to earth were not the same event."

"Mom," said Michael, "were William Miller's followers Adventists? I mean . . . I thought the Seventh-day Adventist Church came along later."

"The Seventh-day Adventist Church *was* formed later," Mother said. "But the word *Adventist* can mean anybody who is eagerly waiting for Jesus to come again. The word *advent* means 'coming.' Jesus' first advent was when He came to earth as a baby at Bethlehem, so we refer to His coming again as His second advent."

"Oh," said Michael, "that makes sense. So anybody who believes in Jesus' soon coming is an Adventist. And that's not the same thing as being a Seventh-day Adventist."

"Right," said Mother.

"OK," said Michael. "Now, what were you saying?"

"I was saying that these early Adventists had learned that the

What Is Jesus Doing Now?

cleansing of the sanctuary and the second coming of Jesus are not the same event. They realized now that there was a sanctuary in heaven. But in order to understand the great disappointment and what had happened, the Adventists needed to figure out what was taking place in the sanctuary and what Jesus was doing there. Let's read a story Jesus told when He was here on earth. It's the story of the wedding garment, and it's found in Matthew 22:2-14."

Michael found the story in his Bible and followed along as mother read:

"The kingdom of heaven is like a king who prepared a wedding feast for his son. The king invited some people to the feast. When the feast was ready, the king sent his servants to tell the people to come. But they refused to come to the feast.

Then the king sent other servants. He said to them, 'Tell those who have been invited that my feast is ready. I have killed my best bulls and calves for the dinner. Everything is ready. Come to the wedding feast.'

But the people refused to listen to the servants. They went to do other things. One went to work in his field, and another went to his business. Some of the other people grabbed the servants, beat them, and killed them. The king was very angry. He sent his army to kill the people who had killed his servants. And the army burned their city.

After that, the king said to his servants, 'The wedding feast is ready. I invited those people, but they were not worthy to come. So go to the street corners and invite everyone you see. Tell them to come to my feast.' So the servants went into the streets. They gathered all the people they could find, both good and bad. And the wedding hall was filled with guests.

Then the king came in to see all the guests. He saw

a man there who was not dressed in the right clothes for a wedding. The king said, 'Friend, how were you allowed to come in here? You are not wearing the right clothes for a wedding.' But the man said nothing. So the king told some servants, 'Tie this man's hands and feet. Throw him out into the darkness. In that place, people will cry and grind their teeth with pain.'

Yes, many people are invited. But only a few are chosen."

Mother closed her Bible. "You see, Michael, before the wedding was to start, the king checked to make sure that the invited guests were wearing their wedding clothes. That's kind of like what Jesus is doing. He has offered us the robe of His goodness, and before He comes and takes us to heaven, He is checking to make sure that all of us who want to go with Him are wearing the garment of His goodness that He gave us."

"That makes sense," said Michael.

"The early Adventists had a lot of questions and didn't understand everything that was happening. They were afraid that the judgment was already over and that no one would be able to change their mind or repent or be converted after that."

"But that wasn't true, was it?" asked Michael. "We can still accept Jesus today and repent."

"Yes, we can," said Mother. "The judgment isn't over yet, and it won't be until Jesus is finished with the work of atonement in the Most Holy Place. In Bible times when the High Priest went into the Most Holy Place on the Day of Atonement, all Israel gathered and prayed and searched their hearts before God to make sure that they weren't hiding any sins. They asked Him to forgive them for anything they had done wrong so they could stand before Him pure and clean."

"Since Jesus is in the Most Holy Place, then we must be living in the time of atonement," Michael said. "That means we should be searching our hearts too."

"Yes," said Mother. "Jesus is still in heaven interceding for us. We need to search our hearts and make sure that we have accepted His robe of goodness, instead of hanging on to any shreds of the old dirty character that we had before Jesus changed us."

"Like muddy clothes," said Michael. "That makes sense. I'm really anxious for Jesus to come again soon. I want to wear His robe of goodness."

"I do too," said Mother.

25

God's
Unchangeable Law

"Michael," said Mother, "today we have something really difficult to study, but it's also really important for us to understand. Do you want to read Revelation 12:7-9, or shall I?"

"I'll read it," Michael said, turning to Revelation in his Bible.

> Then there was a war in heaven. Michael and his angels fought against the dragon. The dragon and his angels fought back. But the dragon was not strong enough. He and his angels lost their place in heaven. He was thrown down out of heaven. (The giant dragon is that old snake called the devil or Satan. He leads the whole world the wrong way.) The dragon with his angels was thrown down to the earth.

"Mom, this makes it really clear that the dragon is Satan."

"And when we know who the dragon is," said Mother, "then we are ready to understand something else. Now read Revelation 13:11."

God's Unchangeable Law

"OK. It says, 'Then I saw another beast coming up out of the earth. He had two horns like a lamb, but he talked like a dragon.' So this is another animal that John saw in vision, and it looked gentle until it opened its mouth," Michael said.

"That's right," said Mother, "but let's stop right there a minute. Before we decide what this gentle-looking animal represents, we need to identify one more animal mentioned in the prophecy. Now would you read Revelation 13:1-10?"

Michael read:

> Then I saw a beast coming up out of the sea. It had ten horns and seven heads. There was a crown on each horn. A name against God was written on each head. This beast looked like a leopard, with feet like a bear's feet. He had a mouth like a lion's mouth. The dragon gave the beast all of his power and his throne and great authority. One of the heads of the beast looked as if it had been wounded and killed. But this death wound was healed. The whole world was amazed and followed the beast. People worshiped the dragon because he had given his power to the beast. And they also worshiped the beast. They asked, "Who is as powerful as the beast? Who can make war against him?"
>
> The beast was allowed to say proud words and words against God. He was allowed to use his power for forty-two months. He used his mouth to speak against God. He spoke against God's name, against the place where God lives, and against all those who live in heaven. He was given power to make war against God's holy people and to defeat them. He was given power over every tribe, people, language, and nation. All who live on earth will worship the beast. These are all the people since the beginning of the world whose names are not written in the Lamb's book of life. The Lamb is the One who was killed.

MICHAEL ASKS WHY

If anyone has ears, he should listen: If anyone is to be a prisoner, then he will be a prisoner. If anyone is to be killed with the sword, then he will be killed with the sword. This means that God's holy people must have patience and faith.

"There sure are a lot of animals in the book of Revelation," said Michael. "It sounds pretty confusing."

"Well," said Mom. "Actually there are only three that we read about in these verses—the dragon, the animal that comes from the land, and the animal that comes from the sea—and we already know that the dragon represents Satan. Now we need to figure out who these other two animals represent. Let's start with the animal that came from the sea—the one to whom the dragon gave his power and authority. A lot of the early Protestants identified this beast as the papacy."

"What's the papacy?" asked Michael.

"The papacy is another word for all the popes—the system of the Roman Catholic Church and its leadership," said Mother.

"Why did these Protestants think this animal represented the papacy?" asked Michael.

"They put this description in Revelation together with something similar that Daniel described in his book. We can read about it in Daniel 7:19-27," Mother replied.

Michael read:

"Then I wanted to know what the fourth animal meant. It was different from all the other animals. It was very terrible. It had iron teeth and bronze claws. It was the animal that crushed and ate what it killed. And it walked on whatever was left. I also wanted to know about the ten horns on its head. And I wanted to know about the little horn that grew there. It had pulled out three of the other ten horns. It looked greater than the others. And it had eyes and a mouth that kept bragging. As I watched, the little horn began making war against God's people. And the horn kept killing them until God, who has been alive forever, came. He judged in favor of the people who belong to the Most High God. And the time came for them to receive the power to rule.

And he explained this to me: 'The fourth animal is a fourth kingdom that will come on the earth. It will be different from all the other kingdoms. It will destroy people all over the world. It will walk on and crush the whole earth. The ten horns are ten kings who will come from this fourth kingdom. After those ten kings are gone, another king will come. He will be different from the kings who ruled before him. He will defeat three of the other kings. This king will say things against the Most High God. And he will hurt and kill God's people. He will try to change times and laws that have already been set. The people that belong to God will be in that king's power for three and one-half years.

'But the court will decide what should happen. And the power of the king will be taken away. His kingdom will be completely destroyed. Then the people who belong to the Most High God will have the power to rule. They will rule over all the kingdoms under heaven with power and greatness. Their power to rule will last forever. And people from all the other kingdoms will respect and serve them.' "

"So, Mom," asked Michael, "who does this animal—the one that Daniel is talking about—represent?"

"Can you think of a powerful empire that took over all the known world and was represented by iron legs in Nebuchadnezzar's dream?"

"Oh, yeah, that would be the Roman Empire."

"So this fourth animal of Daniel's vision represents the Roman Empire," continued Mom. "Then Daniel saw a little horn that grew out of the Roman Empire, but it was somehow different. He described this power as doing some of the same things that the animal did that John saw coming out of the sea in Revelation 13. That's why many Protestant Bible students decided that Revelation 13 and Daniel 7 are talking about the same power."

"But why do people think that Daniel and John are talking about the *papacy?*" Michael wanted to know.

"What does John say this animal will be doing?" asked Mother. "What did you find out about it when you read Revelation 13:1-10 and Daniel 7:19-27?"

"Well," said Michael, "Revelation says it will be speaking against God and making war on God's people. And Daniel says the same thing and that it will try to change God's laws and times."

"That's right" said Mother. "Now who has tried to change God's laws?"

"I'm not sure," said Michael. "How could anyone change one of God's laws?"

"They couldn't, really," said Mother. "But one thing the established church, the Roman Catholic Church, did was to change the day people worshiped from the seventh-day Sabbath to Sunday, the first day of the week. In fact, the Catholic Church admits that they changed the Sabbath to Sunday and that the change demonstrates the pope's power to make such decisions."

"And so that's what Daniel means when he says this power would try to change times and laws that God has already set?" said Michael.

"Yes," said Mother, "the change of the Sabbath to Sunday would be an example of that."

"What does John mean when he says this power would receive a deadly wound?" asked Michael.

"Revelation says that this power will rule for forty-two months, speaking against God and persecuting God's people. Then it would receive a wound that looked like it would be deadly. But the wound would be healed. Do you remember when we talked before, we learned that often a day in Bible prophecy stands for a year of real time?"

"I remember," Michael answered.

"Well, Mother replied, "you add up the time from 538 AD. to 1798—"

"Hang on," said Michael, "what happened in those years, and how do I add that up?"

"The bishop of Rome gained control over all the other church bishops in 538 A.D.," Mother told him. "This put the bishop of Rome, who was also known as the pope, in control of the whole established Christian church in Europe and the west. So if the papacy was to rule for forty-two months, how long would that be?"

"Forty-two times thirty days in each month would be . . . 1,260 days or years," Michael looked up from the paper where he had been writing figures.

"So if the papacy began to rule the church in 538 A.D. and continued for 1,260 years, when would the end of its rule take place?"

"You'd add 538 and 1,260," said Michael. "And the answer is . . . 1798. What happened then?"

"That's when the deadly wound that John talked about happened. The history books tell us that the French army took the pope captive in 1798."

"Oh," said Michael, "he became a prisoner, just like Revelation 13 said."

"But he didn't stay a prisoner forever," said Mother. "OK, now we have identified two of the animals. Let's go on to the animal that came from the earth. Look again at Revelation 13:11. Right after that, another animal—"

"Wait a minute," said Michael, "I want to read that verse from my Bible. Here it is: 'Then I saw another beast coming up out of the earth. He had two horns like a lamb, but he talked like a dragon.' That's the gentle-looking animal with the bad language!"

Mother smiled, "This animal comes out of the earth and grows very quickly. What nation was growing quickly in 1798 and eventually became a great world power?"

"We learned in school that the United States declared it's independence in 1776, so it would be growing fast right about then."

"That's right," said Mother.

"So," said Michael, "do you think this animal with horns like a lamb represents the United States?"

"Yes," said Mother, "that's what I think."

"But one of the reasons people came to America was to have religious freedom," said Michael, "and Revelation 13 says that even though this power looked like a lamb, it spoke like a dragon and made people worship the animal that came from the sea. The United States doesn't do that!"

"No," said Mother, "right now it doesn't."

"So how does this fit in with the lamblike country making people worship the beast?"

"Well," said Mother, "the best way to worship someone is to respect his authority."

"Right," said Michael, "but the United States doesn't have an official church like Europe did in the Dark Ages. And it isn't making people worship the papacy."

"No," Mom said, "it isn't. But by keeping Sunday instead of Sabbath, aren't Protestant churches respecting the authority of the Catholic Church and the authority of the pope to make a change in God's laws?"

"Oh," said Michael, thinking. "Yes, I guess so."

"Mrs. White, who wrote *The Great Controversy,* says that in the future laws will be passed in the United States requiring people to worship on Sunday; we will not be allowed to worship on the seventh-day Sabbath. At that time, those who keep Sunday instead of Sabbath will be worshiping the beast power."

"Oh," said Michael, "that makes sense; I mean, if they know they should worship on Sabbath but obey the law to worship on Sunday, that would be respecting the authority of the Catholic

God's Unchangeable Law

Church over God's law. But I don't see how anyone could ever be forced to do that in this country."

"Not right now," agreed Mother. "People have felt that there could never be religious persecution in this country because the Protestant churches were all so different in their beliefs. But from what John says in the book of Revelation, it certainly seems that toward the end of time Christians will get together and unite on some specific issues—and then there will be persecution."

"I see," said Michael. "So, even though at the time the Bible was written, people in Europe and the Bible lands didn't even know America existed, God still knew it was here and predicted that it would be involved in the end-time conflict."

"That's right," said Mother. "God knows everything that's going to happen. Aren't you glad He told us? With God knowing the end from the beginning, and with us knowing that God is going to win, we never have to be worried about anything."

26

The Seventh-day Sabbath

"Michael," said Mother, "when do you think the Sabbath began?"

"*Uh* . . . a long time ago," said Michael. "Oh, I know! Of course, it began with the creation of the world."

"Yes, in fact, we keep the seventh day holy to honor God as our Creator," agreed Mother. "Why don't you read Genesis 2:1-3?"

"OK." Michael found the text and read:

So the sky, the earth and all that filled them were finished. By the seventh day God finished the work he had been doing. So on the seventh day he rested from all his work. God blessed the seventh day and made it a holy day. He made it holy because on that day he rested. He rested from all the work he had done in creating the world.

"Now read Isaiah 56:1, 2," said Mom.

Michael read, "This is what the Lord says: 'Give justice to all people. Do what is right. Do this because my salvation will come to you soon. Soon everyone will know that I do what is right. The person who obeys the law about the Sabbath will be blessed. And the person who does no evil will be blessed.' " He looked up. "Sabbath was really special, wasn't it?"

"It still is," said Mother. "Adam and Eve kept the Sabbath in the Garden of Eden."

"Noah kept the Sabbath too," said Michael.

"So did Abraham, Isaac, and Jacob," Mother added.

"And Jesus," said Michael.

"Yes. Mrs. White, the author of *The Great Controversy*, tells us that ever since the beginning of time, someone, somewhere, has always kept the Sabbath holy. It was never completely stamped out no matter how strong the people on Satan's side became."

"Always?" asked Michael.

"Always," said Mother. "But Satan tries to keep people from obeying God's laws. Listen to this: 'Then the dragon was very angry at the woman. He went off to make war against all her other children. Her children are those who obey God's commands and have the truth that Jesus taught' "(Revelation 12:17).

"The commandments are very important to God, just like the Sabbath, aren't they," said Michael.

"Yes they are," said Mother. "At different times, people have used different reasons for not wanting to keep the Sabbath. Satan has always helped them come up with an excuse. The early Christians felt that keeping the Sabbath was observing Jewish traditions. Today, people don't want to worship on Sabbath because everyone else worships on Sunday. A change was hard for the early Adventists because people had been keeping Sunday for centuries. People who rejected the Sabbath said to the believers, 'It can't be that you are right and all the educated Bible scholars are wrong.' But as the early Adventists studied the Bible, they discovered two things— the sanctuary and God's law. They realized that the sanctuary and the law went together because in the sanctuary, inside the golden ark of the covenant, right under the lid to the ark, was . . ."

"I know!" said Michael. "The Ten Commandments!"

"That's right," said Mom. "In the heavenly sanctuary, the lid to the ark represented God's throne."

"And the lid was right over His law!" said Michael. "That showed how much God thought of the law."

"That's right," said Mother. "All the dates the early Adventists set for Jesus to come just distracted them from what God really wanted them to learn about the sanctuary in heaven and the importance of His law."

Michael said, "I guess date setting still distracts people, doesn't it?"

"Sometimes," agreed Mom. "Every once in a while you will hear of someone setting a time when they think Jesus is coming again, but Jesus told us nobody would know when He was coming. What God really wants is for us to understand and appreciate what Jesus is doing now."

"And how much He wants us to take His Word seriously," added Michael.

27

Four Keys to Heaven

"What were other churches doing while William Miller was preaching about the Second Coming?" asked Michael.

"During the 1800s," said Mom, "there were lots of revivals. Some were genuine, but many of them were only temporary experiences. People became on fire for the Lord, burned brightly, and burned out quickly, leaving their spiritual life darker than it had been before. Many ministers were preaching that after Jesus died the law wasn't important anymore and that people didn't need to keep it any longer."

"That doesn't make sense," said Michael.

"You're right," said Mom. "If there is no law, then there can be no sin, because sin is just breaking the law."

"Right," said Michael.

"And if there's no sin, then we don't need a Savior."

"Right," said Michael.

"And if there's no need for a Savior, then we wouldn't need Jesus anymore."

MICHAEL ASKS WHY

"Right," said Michael.

"And then pastors wouldn't have anything left to preach about, would they?"

"No," said Michael. "That idea doesn't make any sense."

"In fact," said Mother, "The first step in getting right with Jesus is to realize our sin and how much we need Jesus. The law is like a mirror that helps us do that. It shows us our sins so we will know how much we need Jesus to forgive us.

"There are four keys that unlock the secret of going to heaven with Jesus," explained Mother. "The first key is recognizing that God's law is still important. Jesus said in Matthew 5:17, 'Don't think that I have come to destroy the law of Moses or the teaching of the prophets. I have not come to destroy their teachings but to do what they said.'

"The second key," continued Mother, "is realizing that breaking the law is sin, which means we still need forgiveness."

"Besides," added Michael, "since there is a sanctuary in heaven, it means there must still be a reason for the sanctuary and that people still need to have sins forgiven."

"Yes, and the sanctuary is there for us. We need to use it by confessing our sins, so that Jesus can blot them out in the atonement. That is key number three."

"What's key number four?" asked Michael.

"If a conversion is real, if a person really is sorry for his sins and wants to be forgiven, then there will be a change in that person's life. His experience with God will not be a temporary thing that causes him to burn brightly for a little while and then burn out. It will make a lasting change in his life. Getting to know Jesus makes us different. And the difference should last for the rest of our lives. This change is the evidence that we really know Jesus and that we love Him. That is true conversion and the final key to entering heaven."

"God has made sure we have everything we need, hasn't He?" exclaimed Michael.

28

Grace Covers All

"The Bible tells us there are recording angels who keep track of the choices that we make in life. They write them down in the Book of Remembrance." Mother settled into the chair beside Michael as they began their discussion.

"The angels write down in a book all the choices we make?" asked Michael. "You'd think they would use computers or something!"

Mother laughed. "Maybe they do use computers. Maybe the Bible talked about writing things in a book because people wouldn't understand about computers back when the Bible was written."

"Oh yeah," said Michael. "OK, what does the Bible say about the angels keeping records?"

"Revelation 20:12 says: 'And I saw the dead, great and small, standing before the throne. And the book of life was opened. There were also other books opened. The dead were judged by what they had done, which was written in the books.' Michael, would you read 1 Peter 4:17?"

MICHAEL ASKS WHY

"All right," Michael replied. When he found the text, he read: "It is time for judgment to begin, and it will begin with God's family. If that judging begins with us, what will happen to those people who do not obey the Good News of God?"

"This is telling us that heaven reviews the record of each person's life," said Mother. "All of us have sinned, and the records will show that. However, those who have accepted Jesus' sacrifice as payment for their sins are counted as having no sin at all. Jesus forgives their sins and covers them up, so it's just like they never happened. However, He cannot cover up the sins of people who haven't accepted Him as their Savior or who don't allow Him to control their lives."

"So then," said Michael, "it really matters that we understand Jesus' job so that we can ask Him to cover up our sins, right?"

"Yes," said Mother, "that's right."

"Well," said Michael, "it sounds like what Jesus is doing for us now in heaven is just as important as what He did when He died for us here on earth."

"It is," agreed Mother. "Both His death and His ministry in heaven are necessary to take care of our sins. Sin isn't just bad things we do. Sin can be something no one sees—like letting our heart get separated from God. We can sin, too, by *not* doing things—by not using our abilities for God."

"But all of us sin," said Michael. "How can we be sure our sins are forgiven?"

"Second Corinthians 12:9," said Mother, "assures us that God's grace is more than enough to cover all our sins. We can be sure that if we are sorry and ask Jesus to forgive us that He will. God will always accept the smallest good thing we do if we do it because we love Him. It's important for us to remember, too, that we are saved as individuals and not in groups."

"What does that mean?" asked Michael.

"Well," said Mother, "that means that you are not saved because you belong to a certain church or a certain family. You are saved only if you've asked Jesus to forgive your sins and to cover them up because He died for you."

"Oh," said Michael. "You know, it's kind of scary to think about the judgment and that angels are keeping records of everything we do."

"It can be," agreed Mother. "But remember that if we've accepted Jesus as our Savior and have asked Him to forgive us, then as far as Jesus is concerned, our sins are all gone. He covers us with His perfect robe of righteousness, and we don't have to be scared at all. Jesus is our best Friend."

29

Where Did Sin Come From?

"Mom," said Michael, "I'm kind of confused. Why did God ever let sin happen? I mean, so many people have suffered because of it."

"Yes," said Mother, "they have. The Bible tells us how Lucifer became Satan. Look in Isaiah, chapter 14, verses 13 and 14."

Michael found Isaiah in his Bible and then found chapter 14. He read: "You told yourself, 'I will go up to heaven. I will put my throne above God's stars. I will sit on the mountain of the gods. I will sit on the slopes of the sacred mountain. I will go up above the tops of the clouds. I will be like God Most High.' " "But Mom, that doesn't really tell what happened to Lucifer."

"Yes, it does," Mother countered. "You see, before Lucifer decided he wanted to be like God, he was the highest angel in heaven. He was perfect and beautiful, just the way God created him to be. But Lucifer became impressed with himself. He was filled with pride and thought he was more important than he really was. He was jealous of Jesus, who was God the Son."

Where Did Sin Come From?

"So Jesus was in heaven even before He came to earth as a baby?"

"Oh yes," said Mother. "The first few verses of the book of John tell us that Jesus has always existed with God the Father, long before He came to earth."

"OK," said Michael, "go ahead. Why was Lucifer jealous of Jesus?"

"Lucifer thought he should be included in the plans for the new world God and Jesus were creating. He felt that They were leaving him out on purpose to humiliate him in front of the other angels. Satan became so jealous of Jesus he began talking to the other angels and raising questions—'Why is Jesus involved in the plans for a new world? Why wasn't I included? Why is Jesus honored above me?'

"Lucifer convinced as many angels as he could that God was unfair. Because of his rebellious attitude, he and one-third of the angels were banished from heaven. Now Satan was furious."

"Are Satan and Lucifer the same person?" asked Michael.

"Yes," said Mother. "After he left heaven, he wasn't called Lucifer anymore, because he was no longer a good angel. The name *Lucifer* means 'lightbearer,' and *Satan* means 'the enemy.' "

"OK," said Michael, "so what did Satan do then?"

"He told the other angels it was all God's fault. He claimed it was God's unreasonable rules that had caused him to be jealous and to be banished from heaven. Then he tricked Adam and Eve into sinning. He blamed that on God, too, saying God's rules were not fair to Adam and Eve either. He was shocked when God offered His own Son in exchange for the lives of the humans who had sinned. In everything he did, Satan kept trying to put himself above God."

"Like in the temptation in the wilderness when he asked Jesus to bow down to him or to obey him by doing a miracle and turning the rocks into bread?"

"Yes, that's another example of how he tried to be above God," said Mother. "And when he wasn't able to get Jesus to sin or to acknowledge him as the ruler, he hated Him even more. Finally, he made sure that Jesus was tortured to death."

"That's awful!" said Michael.

"Yes," said Mother, "but it proved to the whole universe, beyond the shadow of a doubt, that God was fair and that He loved humans and was willing to do anything to save them even though Satan had deceived them and made them suffer."

Michael thought about that awhile. Then he said, "If people really understood what happened, there's no way they could blame God for all of the suffering on the earth."

"But so many people don't know," said Mother.

"Someone ought to tell them," said Michael. He sat quietly for several moments. "That's really what this is all about, isn't it?" he said, "proving that God is fair."

"That's what the conflict was about from the beginning," agreed Mother. "The first accusation Satan made was that God was not fair. This great controversy is not about you or me or even about Satan. It's about God and proving that He is fair. And when this war between Christ and Satan is over, everyone will know for sure that God is fair. Everyone will have had an opportunity to choose which side to be on."

"God must love us a lot," said Michael, "to be willing to give us a chance like that!"

"Yes," said Mother. "He's a very loving Father."

"I can't wait until this is all over and everybody understands and loves God," said Michael.

"It will be a great relief to the whole universe when the war ends," said Mother. "But it will also be very sad because some people will never choose to understand. And those people will be lost even though God loves them so much. It will hurt Him terribly to see them die."

"Yes," said Michael, "I guess it will."

"Still," said Mom, "when it is over, then there will be no more

Where Did Sin Come From?

sin because everyone will understand."

"So it will be a happy time but a sad time too," Michael said. "We'll be happy because there is no more sin, but it will be sad that some people choose not to love God and live with Him."

30

Our
Worst Enemy

"Do you know who our worst enemy is?" Mother asked.

"I don't know," said Michael. "Probably we are ourselves."

Mother laughed. "Sometimes that's true," she said. "But actually, Satan is our worst enemy. Would you read Genesis 3:15? This is what God said to Satan after he tricked Adam and Eve into sinning in the Garden of Eden."

Michael found the text and read: "I will make you and the woman enemies to each other. Your descendants and her descendants will be enemies. Her child will crush your head. And you will bite his heel."

"Satan was angry," Mother reminded Michael. "He had been pointing to the fact that Adam and Eve had sinned, to prove that God was unfair, and now God had gone way out of His way to save them. Anyone who was paying attention at all would see that God was loving and merciful. This made Satan hate God even more. He couldn't attack God directly because God is stronger than Satan, of course. But Satan could pick on God's children. So that's what he did, and he is going to keep doing that until this conflict is over. See what Paul says in 2 Timothy 3:2."

"In those times," Michael read, "people will love only themselves and money. They will brag and be proud. They will say evil things against others. They will not obey their parents. People will not be thankful or be the kind of people God wants." He looked up, "But why is there so little resistance to Satan's plan? Why are God's people so, well, *sleepy*? They don't seem to be paying attention."

"Many of God's people are sleepy because they don't have the Holy Spirit in their lives as much as they should. They don't really understand Satan's power and how he plans to fight against God. It's much easier for an enemy to win if the army he is fighting against is asleep. It's easier still if the people don't even know there is a war going on and no one is paying attention. People who don't keep a strong connection with Christ forget these things or never knew about them in the first place.

"People who are close to Jesus hate sin as much as He does. They don't want to do anything that would hurt God because He loves them so much. But many people don't stay connected to God. So they forget that Satan is at war with God's people. They are ignorant of Satan's power and cruelty toward the followers of Jesus. They blame God for evil things that happen. But God isn't the one who causes evil. Bad things happen because there is a war going on and because Satan, the enemy, is so cruel."

"What can we do?" demanded Michael.

"Read Ephesians 6:11, 12," Mother replied.

"Wear the full armor of God," Michael read. "Wear God's armor so that you can fight against the devil's evil tricks. Our fight is not against people on earth. We are fighting against the rulers and authorities and the powers of this world's darkness. We are fighting against the spiritual powers of evil in the heavenly world."

"Now read 1 Peter 5:8," Mother said.

"Control yourselves and be careful! The devil is your enemy.

MICHAEL ASKS WHY

And he goes around like a roaring lion looking for someone to eat."

Mother looked at Michael as he put down the Bible. "Those verses tell us very clearly just who we're fighting against. But we never need to be afraid!"

"Because Jesus fought and won, right?" said Michael.

"That's right," said Mother, "and He will give us strength if we ask. Satan can't control our minds or what we do. He can affect us only if we let him. He can upset us, but he can't destroy us. He can hurt us, but he can never cut us off from Jesus. Satan has already lost the war, but he can still cause us trouble until Jesus comes to take us to heaven."

"I wish Jesus would hurry up!" said Michael.

31

Who Are
the Angels?

"Mom, exactly who are the angels?" asked Michael.

"Look in your Bible, and it will tell you. Try Hebrews 1:14."

Michael read, "All the angels are spirits who serve God and are sent to help those who will receive salvation."

"Now read Psalm 8:5."

"You made man a little lower than the angels. And you crowned him with glory and honor." "So the angels are spirits who serve God and who are sent to help us?" asked Michael.

"Yes," replied Mother. "God created the angels and gave them certain jobs to carry out."

"I remember lots of places in the Bible where there were angels," Michael said. "Like when Daniel was in the lions' den, and angels came to keep him safe. And at Jesus' resurrection an angel came and rolled away the stone and told Him, 'Your Father calls you.' And an angel told Mary she was going to have a baby."

"That's right," said Mother, "and there are many other angel stories in the Bible too. I'm sure you can think of more."

"There's my angel," said Michael, "because every follower of Jesus has a guardian angel."

Mother smiled. "Here are a couple more verses about angels. You read Psalm 34:7, and I'll read Job 1:9, 10."

"All right," Michael said. "The Lord saves those who fear him. His angel camps around them."

Then Mother read, "Satan answered God, 'Job honors God for a good reason. You have put a wall around him, his family and everything he owns. You have blessed the things he has done. So his flocks of sheep and herds of cattle are large. They almost cover the land.' " She looked at Michael. "You see, God uses angels to protect us. I think that wall around Job was a wall of angels."

"But what about that third of the angels who followed Satan? Are they still with him?" Michael wanted to know.

"Unfortunately, yes," said Mother. "Today we refer to them as evil *spirits* because they are on Satan's side. We don't usually call them angels anymore, although the Bible tells us that they can still appear as angels of light. Remember the story in Mark, chapter 5, where there was a man who had evil spirits in him?"

"I thought it was just one evil spirit," said Michael.

"Look at verse 9," said Mother. "When Jesus asked the man's name, he said 'My name is Legion,' because he had so many spirits in him. The Roman legions had anywhere from three thousand to five thousand men, so there must have been thousands of evil spirits in that poor man."

"That's a cool story," said Michael. "I like the part where Jesus sent the spirits out into the pigs, and they all jumped off the cliff into the ocean."

Mother smiled.

"Served the owners right," said Michael. "They shouldn't have been raising pigs anyway. Jews aren't supposed to eat pigs, so why would they raise them and sell them to their friends?"

Mother laughed. "Maybe that's what Jesus thought too. But Satan's spirits always destroy when they inhabit something or some-

Who Are the Angels?

one. The Bible has other stories about evil spirits too. You can read them later in Luke 4:33-36 about the man in the synagogue; or Mark 7:26-30 and Mark 9:17-27, which tell about people who were possessed by evil spirits."

"It sounds as if people who have an evil spirit or a bunch of evil spirits are really suffering and need Jesus to help them."

"They do need Jesus to help them," said Mother, "but they aren't always suffering. Some people have evil spirits because they like them and choose to have them. Simon Magus, the magician, was like that. His story is in the book of Acts.

"Even more dangerous is pretending that Satan doesn't exist at all. If you deny his existence, then you can't protect yourself from his power. Satan really likes it when people describe him as a red devil with horns and beastlike hooves. Then they aren't afraid of him, and they don't pay attention. He is actually a powerful being who's very angry at humans. He is their greatest enemy."

Michael shuddered, "Sounds scary."

"Well Michael," said Mother, "you don't ever have to be afraid of Satan, because Jesus has much more power than Satan will ever have. Jesus puts a hedge of guardian angels around you to keep you safe. He will never let you down. Your part is to renew your friendship with Him each morning and walk with Him throughout the day."

"I certainly will," said Michael.

"Every day I pray for you," said Mother, "putting you in Jesus' hands to keep you safe from Satan's power."

32

God's Word, the Bible

"As we come nearer to the end of time, Satan makes stronger and stronger efforts to tempt us to leave Jesus' side," Mother told Michael as they began their talk.

"You make it sound as if he really plans ahead."

"He does," said Mother. "He makes battle plans just like an army general. Remember the story of Job? Job 1:6 says: 'One day the angels came to show themselves before the Lord. Satan also came with them. The Lord said to Satan, "Where have you come from?" Satan answered the Lord, "I have been wandering around the earth. I have been going back and forth in it." '

"He finds many ways to tempt us to do wrong, and he likes to confuse us if he can. He even tries to use the Bible to confuse people. If a person believes the Bible, then Satan tries to mix him up and get him to twist the Bible around so that he believes it says something it really doesn't say."

"How could Satan use the Bible itself to confuse people?" Michael wanted to know.

God's Word, the Bible

"Sometimes people will take only a single verse, or even just part of a verse, and not pay any attention to all the rest of the chapter. They focus on just that one verse or a few words and claim it means a certain thing. But if they read the whole chapter, they would see it isn't talking about what they think it is at all."

"I'm still not sure I understand," said Michael.

"For example," said Mother, "some people read what Paul wrote in Romans 6:14—'You are not under law but under God's grace'—and say that this proves Christians don't need to obey God anymore, that they don't have to keep God's rules. But if they would read *all* that Paul says in Romans, chapter 6, they would see he is teaching that Christians are saved only by God's grace, not because they earn salvation by being obedient. But that doesn't mean they shouldn't be obeying God's law anymore."

"I see," said Michael. "It's like looking at just part of a picture and thinking that is the whole thing."

"Something like that," agreed Mother. "We need to study the Bible ourselves to know what it says so that we won't be confused by what other people think it means. Also, it's very important for us to pray and ask the Holy Spirit to help us understand by making the Bible plain and clear as we study. Another way Satan tries to confuse people is with science."

"You mean Satan invented science?" asked Michael.

"No!" Mother laughed. "God put the rules of science in place at creation. It's just that people haven't always understood science. They learn a little bit, and when it doesn't agree with what they think the Bible says, then they don't believe the Bible."

"So if they understood more about science," said Michael, "then they would find that science and the Bible actually agree?"

"Of course," said Mother. "God created science, so it will naturally agree with what He tells us in the Bible. Also, we need to be careful what we believe. We will hear a lot of ideas, but they won't always be true. We need to make sure that the Bible backs up everything we believe.

"Satan also likes to tell people that God didn't reveal everything we really need to know. Sometimes people go poking around in places other than the Bible—like talking to spirits—to find out secrets and mysteries that God has never told us. With this temptation, Satan is going back to his lie to Eve in the Garden of Eden when he pretended God was withholding information from her."

"Isn't that called spiritualism?" said Michael.

"Yes," said Mother. "And remember that Satan can appear as an angel of light. Many spiritualists feel that they are being guided by heavenly angels or their inner spirit guide. But we can be sure that we don't need to try to contact spirits; God has already told us in the Bible everything we need to know to be saved.

"Sometimes Satan confuses people by making them doubt whether Jesus was really God. Many of them believe that He was just a good man but not really God. Other people don't believe in a real Satan. Because they don't believe he really exists, they aren't on guard against the things he does to them. Others believe that people don't really die; instead, Jesus takes them to heaven. We will talk more about that next time. Others don't trust God; they doubt His promises. They don't believe that He can really take care of them. But the weakest Christian who trusts Jesus is more than a match for all of Satan's evil angels."

Michael said, "I know in Bible times God protected His people as long as they were loyal to Him by obeying His law. So if we stay on His side today, He'll take care of us too."

"That's right," said Mom. "And remember to talk to Jesus every day, because no one is safe without prayer."

33

Death and Resurrection

"From the very beginning of time, Satan has been confusing people by telling them that there really is no such thing as death. Read in Genesis 3:2-5 what he said to Eve in the garden of Eden." Michael read:

> The woman answered the snake, "We may eat fruit from the trees in the garden. But God told us, 'You must not eat fruit from the tree that is in the middle of the garden. You must not even touch it, or you will die.' " But the snake said to the woman, "You will not die. God knows that if you eat the fruit from that tree, you will learn about good and evil. Then you will be like God!"

"You see," said Mother, "from the time of Adam and Eve, Satan has been trying to convince men and women that they don't really die, that they are naturally immortal."

"What does that mean?" Michael asked.

"It means that Satan has convinced many Christians, and other people, too, that when a person dies, his body dies and is buried, but he has a soul that goes on living somehow—in fact, that his soul *cannot* die and will go on living forever even though the body is dead."

"That doesn't make sense," said Michael.

"A lot of people think it does," said Mother. "Most Christians believe the soul keeps on living forever. That's what immortal means—to keep living forever and never die. Other religions believe that the soul is immortal too—Hindus, Moslems, Buddhists, and others."

"And Satan is the one who started trying to get people to believe that they have a soul that can't die?" asked Michael. "Why would he do that?"

"Because if he can confuse people about this, they will become confused about what God is like. You see, if all humans really live forever, even after they die, then the good people go to live with God, but what about the bad people? Where do they go? If we believe that the soul *can't* die and goes on living forever, then bad people must suffer forever just like the good people enjoy eternal life forever."

"Oh," said Michael, "you're talking about hell now."

"Yes," said Mom. "Many believe that bad people will suffer forever, screaming in pain, being burned in the flames of hell. But God isn't like that."

"Doesn't the Bible talk about hell?" asked Michael.

"Yes, but we have to understand what hell really is and what God is really like. Take a look at what Ezekiel 33:11 says about God."

Michael read, "Say to them: 'The Lord God says: As surely as I live, this is true. I do not want a wicked person to die. I want him to stop doing evil and live. Turn back! Turn back from your wicked ways! You don't want to die, people of Israel.'" "God certainly sounds loving there," said Michael.

Death and Resurrection

"And, of course, He is," said Mother. "But because people believed that sinners burn in hell forever, they became afraid of God, and some became atheists.

"Not everyone fell for Satan's lie about sinners suffering forever in hell. They saw that God would have to be terribly cruel to do such a thing. So then Satan tried to swing these people to the other extreme. He tried to make them believe that God is so gentle and kind that He will save everyone, whether or not they accept Christ's sacrifice. But this isn't true either. The Bible says that the wages of sin is death. Those who choose not to accept Jesus' sacrifice for their sins will have to receive the wages of sin.

"In fact, God knows that those who have chosen Satan as their leader would not be happy in heaven. Think about it. If you had spent your whole life filled with hatred, would you even want to go to heaven and spend eternity with the people you had hated on earth? Heaven would be torture to sinners. They wouldn't like it at all. The Bible tells us very clearly what happens when we die; it says there is a final death for people who don't love God. Here is what Exodus 34:6, 7 says:

> The Lord passed in front of Moses and said, "I am the Lord." The Lord is a God who shows mercy and is kind. The Lord doesn't become angry quickly. The Lord has great love and faithfulness. The Lord is kind to thousands of people. The Lord forgives people for wrong and sin and turning against Him. But the Lord does not forget to punish guilty people.

"And Psalm 145:20 says, 'The Lord protects everyone who loves Him. But He will destroy the wicked.' "

"That's pretty clear," Michael said.

"You understand, don't you, that God is the source of life?" asked Mother.

"Oh yes," said Michael. "He is the only one who can give us

life and keep us alive."

"Right," said mother. "So when everyone has made a final choice about which side to be on, there will be no further reason for God to keep the people alive who have decided not to be with Him. When God withdraws from them, they can no longer live."

Mother continued. "When God destroyed the world in the time of Noah, He was doing it out of mercy to the few good people who were left in the world, because the world had become such a terrible place. If God waited longer, nobody would have been left who was willing to listen to Him. In the same way, God was being merciful when He destroyed Sodom. And when God destroys our world at the end of time, He will also be showing His mercy. He will be ending all sadness and suffering and taking away sin so that there will never be suffering again. Michael, would you read Psalm 9:5, 6?"

Michael read, "You spoke strongly against the foreign nations and destroyed the wicked people. You wiped out their names forever and ever. The enemy is gone forever. You destroyed their cities. No one even remembers them." "That certainly sounds as if there is a definite end to things," said Michael.

"And nowhere," said Mother, "do you read about people writhing in agony, screaming forever, and shouting curses at God for their suffering in eternity. In fact, the Bible says quite clearly that after sin is ended and sinners are destroyed all of us who are left will be praising God forever. It's here in Revelation 5:13. 'Then I heard every living thing in heaven and on earth and under the earth and in the sea. I heard every thing in all these places, saying: "All praise and honor and glory and power forever and ever to the One who sits on the throne and to the Lamb!" ' "

"Satan has convinced many Christians that they go right to heaven when they die. But the Bible teaches that the people who are dead now are just asleep waiting for Jesus to wake them up again."

"We learned a verse in school about that," Michael said. "It's in Ecclesiastes 9:5. It says, 'The living know that they shall die: but the dead know not any thing' " (KJV).

"And verses 6 and 10 add some more to that," Mother said. "After a person is dead, he can no longer show love or hate or jealousy. And he will never again share in the things that happen here on earth. . . . Whatever work you do, do your best. This is because you are going to the grave. There is no working, no planning, no knowledge and no wisdom there."

"Now read Psalm 6:5."

Michael read, "Dead people don't remember you. Those in the grave don't praise you."

"And Psalm 115:17 says, 'Dead people do not praise the Lord. Those in the grave are silent,' " Mother said. "And Psalm 146:4 says, 'When people die, they are buried. Then all of their plans come to an end.' So it's pretty clear from the Bible that when a person dies, he is asleep in the grave; there isn't any soul that keeps on living and knows what is going on.

"If good people went to heaven when they died, and were in heaven for years and years, why would Jesus say he was coming to earth again to resurrect them and give them their reward? They would have already been enjoying their reward for a long time!"

Michael laughed. "That doesn't sound very logical. What would be the point of having a judgment?"

"And how could they live happily in heaven," Mother asked, "while other people—maybe even loved ones—were being tortured in hell? How could they enjoy heaven while watching the pain and struggles of their loved ones left on earth?

"Let's read one more text that tells very clearly what will happen when Jesus comes. Michael, I'll help you find 1 Corinthians 15:52-55, and you read."

It will only take a second. We will be changed as quickly as an eye blinks. This will happen when the last trumpet sounds. The trumpet will sound and those who have died will be raised to live forever. And we will all be changed. This body that will ruin must clothe itself with something that will never ruin. And this body that dies must clothe itself with something that will never die. So this body that ruins will clothe itself with that which never ruins. And this body that dies will clothe itself with that which never dies. When this happens, then this Scripture will be made true: "Death is destroyed forever in victory. Death, where is your victory? Death, where is your power to hurt?"

"It sounds wonderful, doesn't it?" said Mother.

"It will be so exciting," said Michael. "I'll get to hug Grandma Jo and play with my friend Andy who was hit by the car. Grandma Jo will have hair again and won't be sick anymore. And Andy won't be broken."

34

Can the Dead Speak to Us?

"Mom," said Michael. "You remember when Auntie Gina went to that fortuneteller and she said they had seances where they could talk to people who had already died? Can they really do that?"

"No," said Mother. "Ecclesiastes 9:5 says that the dead don't know anything."

"Then who do those people speak to? Aunt Gina said the people at the seance were talking to someone."

"Satan is able to make himself look like dead friends and loved ones," Mother replied, "so that people will actually recognize them. Because he is a spirit, he can take any form he wants to."

"So when people think they are talking to a friend who has died, they are really talking to Satan or one of his angels?"

"Yes. We call that kind of communication *spiritualism*. Those who believe in spiritualism believe that humans don't really die but go on living throughout eternity. They think people just keep progressing, getting better and better, and eventually become gods."

"That sounds like what Satan told Eve in the Garden of Eden," said Michael.

"It does, doesn't it?" said Mother. "Satan told her, 'God knows that if you eat the fruit from that tree, you will learn about good and evil. Then you will be like God!' Because of this lie, God later made strong rules against witchcraft for Israel, so that the Israelites would not be confused. They were not supposed to allow any witches to live in their country or practice witchcraft anywhere near them. You can read about it in Leviticus 19:31."

Michael looked up the text and read, "Do not go to mediums or fortune-tellers for advice. If you do, you will become unclean. I am the Lord your God."

"I remember the story about the witch of Endor and how King Saul went to talk to her because he was worried about how the battle would go the next day. He actually saw something that looked like the prophet Samuel. But you're saying it wasn't really Samuel?"

"Yes," said Mother. "Samuel was dead."

"But the person that King Saul saw told him he was going to die in the battle the next day, and that came true."

"That's right. But Satan knows what his plans are for the next day, and unless God keeps them from happening, Satan can predict what he's going to do. So fortunetellers often are correct in their predictions, but they are still being led by Satan, and we should stay away from them."

"I guess so," said Michael. "With Satan as cruel as he is, we should stay as far away from him as possible."

"Just remember," said Mother, "Satan can control us only if we choose to give in to his temptations. God is always there to protect us as long as we ask Him to."

35

Tradition
or the Bible?

"Mom," said Michael, "in some of the history stories, the
Catholic Church really persecuted people. They burned Protestants and other people at the stake and tortured them to death. But
they don't do that now. Catholics and Protestants seem to be pretty
good friends."

"Yes," said Mother, "there isn't the same kind of persecution
going on today. But let's talk about why such things happened. You
see, Protestants placed a high value on liberty. They wanted to be
free to worship as they believed. It was so important to them that
they were willing to die for it. The church leaders who persecuted
them claimed infallibility."

"What is that?" asked Michael.

"Infallibility means they could never make a mistake."

"You mean they tried not to make mistakes?"

"No," said Mom, "when they claimed infallibility, they meant
that they never had made a mistake and never would."

"Wow," said Michael, "Everybody makes mistakes. God is the

only One who is really perfect like that."

"And," said Mother, "if the Catholic Church believes that persecuting people in the past was not a mistake, then what is to stop it from persecuting people again? Some people say that persecution happened back then because everyone was more cruel than people are today and they didn't think anything was wrong with killing people who didn't agree with them about religious things. They say that only people who are prejudiced against Catholics would suggest that persecution could ever happen again in our day. They point out that the constitution of the United States promises liberty of conscience. But listen to what Pope Pius IX had to say: 'The absurd and erroneous doctrines or ravings in defense of liberty of conscience are a most pestilential error—a pest, of all others, most to be dreaded in a state.' "

"But there are good people like Aunt Pat in the Catholic Church," said Michael.

"Of course there are," said Mother. "God has His faithful people in all Christian churches. Wonderful Catholics like Mother Teresa helped many needy people. There is a lot that is attractive about the Catholic Church. But God wants us to pay attention to what He has said in the Bible, no matter what others may say or do.

"The Catholic leadership and the Jewish church of Jesus' time are a lot alike in many ways. The Jewish church of Jesus' time honored the law; the Catholics honor the cross. The symbol of the cross means a lot to Catholics; they use it in their churches and even on their clothes. The Catholic Church considers tradition to be just as important as God's law or what He says in the Bible—maybe even more important."

"What does 'tradition' mean?" Michael asked.

"Traditions are things we believe or do just because we've always believed them or done them that way or because they have been around a long time."

"So how does the Catholic Church put traditions above the Bible?"

Tradition or the Bible?

"For one thing," said Mother, "the church claims that priests can forgive people's sins. That's why Catholics confess their sins to the priest. They also pray to saints—good people who lived long ago—and to Mary, Jesus' mother. They have statues and images in their churches of the saints and apostles."

"But none of that is in the Bible," Michael said.

"No," agreed Mother. "That is why they are putting traditions above the Bible when they follow such practices. And, of course, they claim that the church changed the Sabbath from the seventh day of the week to the first day—Sunday—and that tradition, in this case, overrules the Bible.

"But by following such traditions, even though they have paid a lot of attention to details, they have misrepresented God's character. They have made Him come across to the people as cruel as Someone who would crush human liberty instead of Someone who was willing to die so that each person could freely choose to serve Him or not.

"Protestants protested against many of these unbiblical traditions in the Catholic Church. That's how they got their name, by protesting. But today, many Protestant churches are becoming more like the Catholic Church and are also putting tradition above God's law. Especially when Protestants follow the Catholic Church in observing Sunday instead of Saturday, it would be very easy for persecution to start over this issue."

Michael looked solemn. "I think we ought to do what God says no matter what human traditions say."

36

Trouble in the Future

"Mom," Michael said, "yesterday you told me that persecution might come in the future. How could that happen?"

"That's a good question, Michael," Mother replied. "I'm glad you are thinking about the things we're discussing. We are fortunate that God has told us ahead of time what will happen. That way we can be prepared instead of surprised. Satan has long planned to overthrow God's law and to deceive and confuse as many people as possible. He wants them to believe that God's law is unfair. Early in the history of the church, he introduced all kinds of errors into Christian teachings.

"Truth and error came into conflict, and Christians had to choose between following God's laws or human rules. They had to decide whether to believe what the Bible teaches or human traditions. The world has often made fun of people who believe that the Bible is true and should be followed. Satan influenced church leaders to call them fanatics who weren't smart enough to understand the real meaning of the Bible. He also influenced church leaders to say that God's law had been done away with."

"But that doesn't make sense," said Michael. "No government, even here on earth, can operate without laws. How could people think that God's government could exist without laws?"

"It doesn't have to make sense," said Mother. "If Satan can convince people that God's laws aren't important, then they won't have to keep them. It's much easier for people to believe that God's laws are done away with than to be obedient to them."

"But remember when we were talking about what happened in France?" said Michael. "They abolished God's laws, and people were dishonest and stole things. People couldn't trust each other."

"When God's laws were disregarded in France," said Mother, "human life was unimportant; lots of people were killed. Marriage wasn't sacred anymore. Children were disobedient. The whole country was filled with violence; even the courts and judges were unfair. Who would want to live in a country like that? But people don't think about those things when they ignore God's laws and the way God has told us to live. People think they know better than God."

"So if Satan couldn't keep people from having Bibles," said Michael, "I guess he decided to persuade them that the Bible wasn't important."

"Satan has focused on two areas—what happens when a person dies and Sabbath keeping," said Mother. "If people don't understand what happens when a person dies, then they can be easily fooled by spiritualism to believe that people go on living and can communicate with them some way. And if people don't understand God's law about keeping the Sabbath, church leaders can deceive them when they claim that His law isn't important anymore."

"Like the Catholic Church did back in the Dark Ages?" Michael wanted to know.

"Yes," said Mother, "but it isn't just Catholics. A lot of Christians don't understand these things. We need to pray for anyone whom Satan has confused about Sabbath keeping or who feels that God's law is not important. Many simply have never read what the Bible says about these things; they just don't understand.

"Church leaders are especially responsible. They have taught the people things that aren't true. Because of this, Satan will be able to deceive many Christians. Someday, Protestants, who once valued freedom so much, will join hands with spiritualism. They will cooperate with the Catholic Church and agree that it did have authority to change the Sabbath from the seventh day to the first day of the week.

"Miracles will unite Protestants, spiritualists, and Catholics. They will believe that the whole world is about to be converted and that a wonderful time is coming when everyone will worship together and there will be a single world government and a single world church."

"Wow," said Michael. "That sounds like some of the things I've heard on TV about a New World Order."

"Yes," said Mother. "A long time ago God told us what was going to happen. Now some of these things are actually taking place. And more people will be deceived as they see miracles and healings taking place.

"Satan will also spend lots of time figuring out how he can use the laws of science and nature to cause terrible disasters. The more people turn away from God, the less God will be able to protect them. So Satan will be able to cause more disasters and diseases. There will be terrible accidents on land and sea."

"And in the air," said Michael. "On the news we see airplanes crashing sometimes."

"And it will get worse, said Mother. "Tornadoes and hailstorms, floods and cyclones, tidal waves and earthquakes, and famines and air pollution. Read what Isaiah 24:4, 5 says."

Michael read, "The earth will dry up and die. The world will grow weak and die. The great leaders in this land will become weak. The people of the earth have ruined it. They do not follow God's teachings. They do not obey God's laws. They break their agreement with God that was to last forever." He looked up. "That sounds scary, like the world is going to get to be a terrible place."

"But when things get bad, we can always trust God to be with us," Mother assured him. "No matter what happens, He won't ever leave us alone. He's promised to be with us to the very end of the world, and He always keeps His promises.

"But the Bible does say that some terrible things will happen before Jesus comes," Mother went on. "For example, disasters will get worse and worse. As a result, people will begin saying that the whole world needs to turn to God and worship Him. But they will be teaching that everyone should worship on Sunday. And as these terrible disasters continue, they are going to look for someone to blame."

"So you're saying that it would be easy for them to blame anyone who didn't agree with them and their ideas about worship and one world church?"

"Exactly," said Mother.

"It's sort of like that Bible story you read me," said Michael. "The one about Ahab. You remember when he and Jezebel had been so bad and God caused a drought in Israel. It hadn't rained for three years. When Ahab ran into Elijah, he said 'So you're the one that's been causing all these problems,' when really it was Ahab and his wife, Jezebel, who had been causing the problems."

"Yes. Just like in Ahab's day, Satan will try to confuse people. And if he can't confuse someone, he will try to *force* that person to follow him. Those who keep the Bible Sabbath will be accused of disobeying the government. Ministers and leaders will preach from the pulpit that God wants them to obey the government. They will misrepresent and condemn people who are faithful to God's commandments."

"It sounds terrible," said Michael.

"It will be a difficult time," said Mother, "but Jesus has promised that He will be with us always, and we will never ever be left alone through any of those hard times. He will be with us just as He was with Elijah or Daniel."

37

Safety in the Scriptures

"Last night we talked about the hard times that are coming," Michael said. He looked very serious. "What can we do to get through them and stay on Jesus' side?"

"Fortunately, God has given us good instruction in the Bible," Mother replied. "It will keep us safe if we follow it."

"Do you mean that if we follow what God says in the Bible we won't get hurt in any of the disasters that will happen?" Michael asked.

"No," said Mother. "I'm sure God will do all He can to keep us safe physically. But sometimes good people get hurt. I'm talking about God keeping us safe spiritually. If we choose to follow Him, He will help us to follow even more closely.

"Of course, Satan does everything he can to keep people from learning what the Bible teaches. He creates counterfeits to make it hard to tell the difference between what God actually taught and what men say that God taught. In order to stay faithful to Him during the coming trials, we need to understand for ourselves what the Bible teaches. Mrs. White says we need to 'fortify our minds' with the truths of the Bible to be safe spiritually. What do you think of when you think of a fortified city?"

Michael thought awhile. "It would need to have a strong wall and good soldiers, wouldn't it?"

"Yes," agreed Mother. "And what would it need to have stored inside the walls?"

"Oh yeah," smiled Michael, "the city wouldn't last very long without a supply of food and water."

"Right," said Mother. "What could the wall and the soldiers represent in the 'fortified city' of our minds?"

"Maybe the wall would be like God's law that protects us, and the soldiers might represent the angels," Michael replied.

"I think you're right," responded Mother. "And what would the supplies inside the city represent?"

"Would that be like knowing the Bible for ourselves?"

"It certainly would. If we are to keep from being deceived, we need to have real Bible information stored in our minds. Otherwise, we would just believe our feelings or whatever other people tell us, whether or not they are in harmony with God's Word."

Michael said, "It sounds as though we need to make sure we take time to learn things *now* that we'll need to remember *then*."

"That's what we've been doing as we've talked about these things," said Mother. "And we need to be sure to invite Jesus into our hearts every day. Let's look at some Bible verses now. Would you read Revelation 14:9?"

"OK," said Michael. "A third angel followed the first two angels. This third angel said in a loud voice: 'It will be bad for the person who worships the beast and his idol and gets the beast's mark on the forehead or on the hand.' " "What is the mark of the beast, Mom, and how do we keep from getting it? What does it look like? Is it like a tattoo or something?"

"No," smiled Mother. "The mark of the beast isn't anything you can see; it isn't like a tattoo actually written on someone's body.

The mark of the beast is the way the Bible describes people accepting the special deceptions of Satan in the last days. It says that those who choose to follow Satan and his rules, instead of God and His rules, will be 'marked' as unfaithful to God. People who follow what their church leaders teach them, instead of studying in the Bible for themselves, will be 'marked' as unfaithful."

"Does that mean that we shouldn't trust any of our church leaders?" asked Michael.

"No," said Mother. "Most of our church leaders are wonderful, godly people, but we are all responsible for studying our Bibles. We all need to make sure that what we believe is what God said. People will have to make hard choices because sometimes their loyalties will be divided. Maybe some members of their own family, people they love and good friends, will choose the wrong way. But Jesus will help us. Psalm 16:7, 8 promises, 'I praise the Lord because he guides me. Even at night, I feel his leading. I keep the Lord before me always. Because he is close by my side I will not be hurt.' That's an encouraging promise, isn't it? And I really like the prayer that David prayed in Psalm 119:18. 'Open my eyes to see the wonderful things in your teachings.' "

"That's a good promise," said Michael. "I think I'll pray that prayer too."

"Here's another helpful promise," said Mother. "It's John 14:26. 'But the Helper will teach you everything. He will cause you to remember all the things I told you. This Helper is the Holy Spirit whom the Father will send in My name.' "

"That's great! So God will help us remember Bible verses when we need them. What else can I do to get ready?" asked Michael.

"Take a look at Psalm 119:11," suggested Mother.

Michael found the text and read: "I have taken your words to heart so I would not sin against you." "What does this mean, Mom?"

"It means that if we really listen to God's Word and think about it, and believe it, it will help us not to sin. Too many people today look for easy meanings in the Bible, or they just ignore it completely. We need to accept what it says and put it into practice. We still have a choice about whom to follow. This text is talking about choosing to follow God's Word and being obedient.

"Many people today say it doesn't matter what we believe as long as we do what we think is right. But that isn't true. For example, suppose you're traveling and you come to an intersection where two roads go off in different directions. A sign points down one road to the place you want to go. But you ignore the sign and take the road that "seems right" to you. You may mean well, but you will still be on the wrong road and end up in the wrong place.

"Here's another verse about choosing. Read John 7:17."

Michael read, "If anyone chooses to do what God wants, then he will know that my teaching comes from God. He will know that this teaching is not my own."

"Does this mean that God will help us to know what is right if we choose to follow Him?"

"That's exactly what it means," said Mother.

"I'm glad God has given us these promises," said Michael. "How could anyone be lost with all the help God has promised to give us?"

"It's hard to understand," said Mother, "and I'm sure it makes God cry when He thinks about it."

"Well, I don't want Him to ever have to cry about me. I love Him too much for that. I'm going to prepare for this time by staying on His side and storing His word in my heart and mind."

"I'm sure that will make God very happy," said Mother. "And He wants us to do all we can to be ready. But just remember that it is Jesus who saves us. It really isn't how good we are or how much Bible we know."

"I know," said Michael. "But I still want to show Him I love Him by doing whatever I can to be ready when He comes."

38

Choosing to Be Loyal

"Michael, do you know what the word *prophecy* means?" asked Mother.

"Sure. When God wanted to send a message to people, He used a prophet. If it was an important message, He sent it to a major prophet. If it was just a little message, God sent it to a minor prophet."

Mother smiled. "Actually," she said, "all of God's messages are important. The prophets we call 'major' prophets wrote longer books than the ones we call 'minor' prophets—that's all. But you're right that people who receive messages from God are called *prophets*. And the messages they receive are called *prophecy*.

"Most of the prophecies in the Bible have already happened. Today we are going to talk about some prophecies that haven't happened yet. Please read Revelation 18:1, 2, and 4."

Michael read:

> Then I saw another angel coming down from heaven. This angel had great power. The angel's glory made the

earth bright. The angel shouted in a powerful voice: "The great city of Babylon is destroyed! She has become a home for demons. She has become a city for every evil spirit, a city for every unclean and hated bird." ... Then I heard another voice from heaven say: "Come out of that city, my people, so that you will not share in her sins. Then you will not receive the terrible things that will happen to her."

"By the time this prophecy takes place, the religious world will be in a terrible condition," said Mother. "There will be spiritualism and disobedience throughout the churches."

"Spiritualism means not believing that the dead are really dead, doesn't it?" asked Michael.

"That's right," said Mother.

"A lot of people believe that the dead can come back as angels and help them with things. I've seen TV shows about that."

"Yes," said Mother, "many people do believe that. But we know from what the Bible says that the dead are unconscious and can't take part in anything that is going on here on earth."

"And the disobedience that will be in the churches at the end of time means that they won't be keeping all of God's commandments, especially the one about the Sabbath, right?"

"Yes," replied Mother. "Most churches believe that we should obey God's commandments—except the fourth one. As this condition progresses, people who choose to follow the beast instead of Jesus will receive the mark of the beast."

"And the beast is Satan?" interrupted Michael.

"Yes," said Mother. "Satan and the institutions through which he works. So those who choose not to follow God but to do things their own way—or Satan's way—will receive his mark."

"OK, I've got it," said Michael. "And the mark of the beast isn't some kind of real mark on people's skin, right?"

"No," Mother replied, "it isn't. The mark of the beast is the sign of those who are loyal to the power that is fighting against God. So those who follow the beast power are 'marked' as disloyal to God. But John also says in Revelation that those who remain faithful to God receive His seal. They are 'marked' too; marked as faithful to God. As this process continues, countries will use civil penalties to try to make everybody worship the same way and on the same day—Sunday."

"Civil penalties? Do you mean like fines or sending people to jail or things that are decided in court?" asked Michael.

"Yes," said Mother. "When all of this happens, the Sabbath will become the biggest test of loyalty to God. The question will become: Will we be faithful to God and obey His commandment to keep the seventh-day Sabbath holy? Or will we obey Satan and worship on the first day of the week? Everyone will have a chance to make the right choice. No one will be punished by God until he or she understands truth and decides to reject it anyway.

"The United States started out being a defender of religious freedom, but it will become more and more intolerant of religious differences. In every generation, God has sent prophets to remind people to return to Him, and to point out people's sins."

"And no one likes having their sins pointed out!" Michael said.

"That's why most of God's prophets have been rejected and badly treated by some people," agreed Mother.

"Well then," said Michael, "I suppose God's people will be treated badly at the end of time, too, if they have to point out when people are not following God."

"Yes," said Mother, "I'm afraid that's how it will go. But when they are taken to court and when they are accused, they will just answer: 'Can you show us from the Word of God what our mistake is?' "

"But the Bible is clear," said Michael, "so the people accusing them won't be able to point out mistakes."

"But many people are not familiar with what the Bible says," Mother continued. "Also, there will be people during this time who have known the Bible and the prophecies. Once they belonged to God's people, but they haven't been faithful to God in their hearts. Now they will join with the people who are accusing God's followers.

"That's terrible," said Michael. "How could they leave and go to the other side?"

"Not everybody is fully committed to God," Mother replied. "Some people are obedient on the outside but not on the inside. These people will be some of the most effective persecutors of God's people. They will be afraid of the punishments that are being passed out to God's people, and they will join those who are persecuting them.

"Meanwhile, God's people will be going through a very hard time. They will be worried that perhaps their mistakes have caused some of their problems. They will keep wondering, 'Is this our fault? Have we done something to give God a bad reputation?' They will say, 'If we had understood the consequences, we never would have said anything about the sins in the world.' But, of course, they must do what they know is right and leave the results with God.

"And God will give them strength and will increase their faith so that they will be able to face everything that they need to. As long as Jesus remains in the sanctuary working as our Intercessor, the Holy Spirit will be able to restrain evil on the earth. It won't be nearly as bad as it might have been otherwise."

"So the Holy Spirit will still be helping us?"

"Yes," said Mother, "The Bible promises us extra help from the Holy Spirit during this time. It refers to this help as 'the latter rain' because in Bible times they had the early rains in the spring and then the later rains right before the harvest. You can read about that in Joel 2:23."

Michael read, "So be happy, people of Jerusalem. Be joyful in the Lord your God. He will do what is right and will give you rain. He will send the early rain and the late rain for you, as before."

"And you can also read in Acts 2:17, 21 about the way God will help us."

Michael found that text too and read, "God says: 'In the last days I will give my Spirit freely to all kinds of people. Your sons and daughters will prophesy. Your old men will dream dreams. Your young men will see visions. . . . Then anyone who asks the Lord for help will be saved.' "

"So when the Holy Spirit's help is poured out in extra quantities on God's people, many wonderful things will happen," Mother said. "There will be great miracles among God's people. But Satan will also be able to perform miracles. This can be very confusing to people who haven't studied carefully what the Bible teaches. That's why it's so important to study the Bible now so we can be ready for the time we've been talking about."

"I want to be ready," Michael said. "And I'm glad God promises us special help for the hard times."

39

A Time
of Trouble

"Mom," Michael said, "tell me about the time of trouble. We talked a little bit about it at school, and it makes me afraid."

"All right. Let's start with some Bible verses. First, read what the angel said to Daniel in chapter 12:1."

Michael found the chapter in Daniel and read, "Daniel, at that time Michael, the great prince, will stand up. (He is the one who protects your people.) There will be a time of much trouble. It will be the worst time since nations have been on earth. But your people will be saved. Everyone whose name is written in God's book will be saved."

"Another good verse is Revelation 22:11."

"Whoever is doing evil, let him continue to do evil. Whoever is unclean, let him continue to be unclean. Whoever is doing right, let him continue to do right. Whoever is holy, let him continue to be holy," Michael read.

"These two verses are talking about the close of probation," said Mother.

MICHAEL ASKS WHY

"What is the 'close of probation'?" asked Michael.

"Ever since Adam and Eve sinned, about six thousand years ago," said Mother, "everyone has had the opportunity to choose whether to be on God's side or on Satan's side. This has been a period of 'probation' when people were deciding whom they would follow. But just before Jesus returns, everyone who is alive at that time will make a final choice. No one will be left who hasn't made up his or her mind which side to be on. This is called the 'close of probation,' and it will close because everyone has made a final decision.

"Jesus' work will be all finished in the heavenly sanctuary because God's people will now be sealed as righteous. They will 'continue to be holy,' just as you read in Revelation 22:11. Those who have decided to go against God's laws have made a permanent choice too. They will 'continue to do evil.' Then the Holy Spirit will be removed from the earth."

"That sounds scary," said Michael. "Remember in the story of Moses in Egypt how just one angel came through Egypt and killed all the firstborn sons in the whole country? If one *good* angel could do that, just think what trouble a whole bunch of *evil* angels could cause in the world—especially if the Holy Spirit wasn't there to keep things in check!"

"It will be a terrible disaster," said Mother.

"Will God's people be blamed for all the problems?" Michael wanted to know.

"Yes," said Mother. "The time of trouble will be a terrible time for the world. Especially for God's enemies, but it will be a hard time for God's people, too, in a different way. Read Jeremiah 30:5-7."

Michael found Jeremiah and read, "This is what the Lord said: 'We hear people crying from fear. They are afraid. There is no peace. Ask this question, and consider it: A man cannot have a baby. So why do I see every strong man holding his stomach in pain like a woman having a baby? Why is everyone's face turning white like a dead man's face? This will be a terrible day! There will never be another time like this. This is a time of great trouble for the people of Jacob. But they will be saved from it.' " "What does Jeremiah mean by 'trouble for the people of Jacob'?" asked Michael.

"Remember in the story of Jacob," said Mother, "that his trouble came at night while he and his family were trying to go back home. His brother, Esau, was coming to meet him with a huge army. Jacob sent his family across a stream and then wrestled all night with doubts and worries. He felt that all his troubles were his own fault for the mistakes that he had made in the past."

"Well, he did make some big ones!" said Michael.

"Yes," said Mother, "he did. And now he was defenseless. He was wondering if his family would be killed. He confessed everything to God. He repented."

"That means he was sorry, right?" asked Michael.

"Yes," said Mother. "He was hanging onto the Lord as His only defense. Without God's protection, he and his family would be killed. Jacob told God that he couldn't let Him go unless He blessed him."

"Oh, I see," said Michael. "That's how it will be for God's people at the end of time. They will be defenseless and afraid that they will be killed unless God takes care of them. And they'll be worried about things they have done earlier; they'll be wondering, like Jacob, if it's their fault that they're having all these problems."

"Yes," said Mother. "Satan claimed he had the right to destroy Jacob because of his sin. As you said, Michael, Jacob had made some big mistakes. He was very aware of his weakness and the wrong things he had done."

Michael looked thoughtful. "So, like Jacob, God's people at this time will really need assurance of forgiveness from God? And they will be worried that things they have done will hurt God's reputation?"

"Yes," said Mother. "Isaiah 27:5 says, 'If anyone comes to me for safety and wants to make peace with me, he should come and make peace with me.' It's important for God's people not to lose courage and hope, even though their prayers are not immediately answered. We need to remember that if we ask Jesus to take away all our sins and forgive them, He will. He promised in 1 John 1:9—"

"I know that verse," said Michael. "Let me say it. 'But if we confess our sins, he will forgive our sins. We can trust God. He does what is right. He will make us clean from all the wrongs we have done.'"

"Good!" said Mother. "We need to confess our sins now and accept Jesus' pardon. Then in the time of trouble, even though we will feel bad about the many poor choices we have made, we won't be able to think of even one unforgiven sin.

"Other things will happen during this difficult time too. The Bible tells us that people will come along claiming to be Christ. Read Matthew 24:23-25."

"At that time," Michael read, "someone might say to you, 'Look, there is the Christ!' Or another person might say, 'There he is!' But don't believe them. False Christs and false prophets will come and perform great things and miracles. They will do these things to the people God has chosen. They will fool them, if that is possible. Now I have warned you about this before it happens."

"Mrs. White tells us that Satan will imitate Jesus' coming," said Mother. "And he will tell people that he changed the Sabbath to Sunday and that the people who are still hanging on to the old Jewish Sabbath are causing all the problems in the world. But one thing Satan cannot imitate. He cannot come in the clouds as Jesus has promised to do. He will appear in different spots on earth, but He cannot come so that every eye in the whole world can see him at once."

"But Jesus can do that," said Michael.

"Yes, Revelation 1:7 tells us about that. 'Look, Jesus is coming with the clouds! Everyone will see him, even those who stabbed him. And all peoples of the earth will cry loudly because of him. Yes, this will happen! Amen.' Now, Michael, you read

A Time of Trouble

1 Thessalonians 4:16, 17."

Michael read, "The Lord himself will come down from heaven. There will be a loud command with the voice of the archangel and with the trumpet call of God. And those who have died and were in Christ will rise first. After that, those who are still alive at that time will be gathered up with them. We will be taken up in the clouds to meet the Lord in the air. And we will be with the Lord forever."

"In Matthew 24:27 Jesus Himself described His coming so that we would know exactly what will happen." "When the Son of Man comes, he will be seen by everyone. It will be like lightning flashing in the sky that can be seen everywhere."

"All of that sounds real good, Mom. But the things that happen *before* Jesus comes in the clouds . . . well, they don't sound very good."

"It's true that God's people will go through a hard time before Jesus comes. Some of them will be in prison, and some of them will be hungry and treated badly. But God will not forget them. In fact, although it's easy now to worry about the difficult times ahead, when they actually arrive, God's people will be much more concerned about spiritual things than the physical hardships. They will want to be sure that they have repented of all their sins and that they are all forgiven."

"I know God never forgets us," said Michael. "Joseph was in prison and treated badly, but God didn't forget him. He became the ruler of Egypt."

Mother smiled.

"And God didn't forget Noah during the Flood. He didn't forget Daniel when he was thrown into the lions' den. And He didn't forget Elijah when he was hungry by the Brook Cherith."

"And He won't forget us," said Mother. "Read Isaiah 49:14-16."

"Jerusalem said, 'The Lord has left me. The Lord has forgotten me.' The Lord answers, 'Can a woman forget the baby she nurses? Can she feel no kindness for the child she gave birth to? Even if she could forget her children, I will not forget you. See, I have written your name on my hand. Jerusalem, I always think about your walls.' "

"In that text, *Jerusalem* represents God's people. They may think God has forgotten them, but He never will. Mrs. White tells us that although enemies may put God's people in prison, they won't be able to cut them off from communicating with God. She says that angels will come to God's people as they're in their prison cells and will cheer them up and bring them songs in the night to encourage them."

"That makes things sound a lot better," said Michael.

"Other things will be happening in the world too. Revelation describes plagues that will come on the earth. One plague will be the sun becoming very hot. Read what Revelation 16:8, 9 says about that."

Michael read, "The fourth angel poured out his bowl on the sun. The sun was given power to burn the people with fire. They were burned by the great heat, and they cursed the name of God. God is the One who had control over these troubles. But the people refused to change their hearts and lives and give glory to God."

"Now read Joel 1:10-12."

"The fields are ruined. Even the ground is dried up. The grain is destroyed. The new wine is dried up. And the olive oil runs out. Be sad, farmers. Cry loudly, you who grow grapes. Cry for the wheat and the barley. Cry because the harvest in the field is lost. The vines have become dry. And the fig trees are dying. The pomegranate trees, the date palm trees and the apple trees have dried up. All the trees in the field have died. And the happiness of the people has died, too."

Then Mother found Amos 8:3 and read, " 'On that day the palace songs will become funeral songs,' says the Lord God. 'There will be dead bodies thrown everywhere!' " "So you see what a wreck the earth will become."

"How can anyone stay alive through all of this?" Michael wanted to know.

A Time of Trouble

"Mrs. White tells us that these plagues will not be happening everywhere at the same time," said Mother. "So although they will all happen somewhere, they won't all be happening to the whole world."

"Oh," said Michael. "Maybe one place will have an earthquake and another place will have a famine, and so on."

"Right," said Mother. "Habakkuk 3:17, 18 tells us what our attitude should be during this time. 'Fig trees may not grow figs. There may be no grapes on the vines. There may be no olives growing on the trees. There may be no food growing in the fields. There may be no sheep in the pens. There may be no cattle in the barns. But I will still be glad in the Lord. I will rejoice in God my Savior.' "

"That's a good encouragement text," said Michael. "We should make a big poster of that so all of God's people can hang it up in their rooms and learn it."

"That's a very good idea," Mother said. "Other special Bible texts that will help us during this hard time are Psalm 91 and Psalm 127. In fact, it would be good to memorize these two Psalms; they can get us through many difficult times."

"With all of these terrible things happening," said Michael, "the world is going to come to an end pretty fast, isn't it?"

"Yes," said Mother. "Mrs. White tells us that the end will come more quickly than most people expected. But God's people will be safe. Listen to Psalm 27:5 from the *New International Version*. 'For in the day of trouble he will keep me safe in his dwelling; he will hide me in the shelter of his tabernacle and set me high upon a rock.' God's advice is to come hide with Him in His tabernacle during these hard times."

"How do we do that?" asked Michael. "Moses' tabernacle isn't around anymore. And neither is the temple the Jews built in Jerusalem."

"You're right," said Mother. "You have studied your history! But there's a heavenly sanctuary too. And no matter where we are or what kind of trouble we are in, we can close our eyes, and inside

173

our minds we can be in the heavenly sanctuary with Jesus. We can hide there with Him no matter what is going on around us."

"That's neat," said Michael. "What a cool way to hide!"

40

Jesus
Is Coming!

"During all our hard time," began Mother, "God has promised us a song in the night."

"Does that mean we'll be happy even in terribly bad times?" said Michael.

"Well," said Mother, "at least it means that God will give us courage. Isaiah 30:29 says, 'You will sing happy songs as on the nights you begin a festival. You will be happy as people listening to flutes as they go to the mountain of the Lord. The Lord is the Rock of Israel.' "

"But how will we be able to sing happy songs during such awful experiences?" asked Michael. "Even if God is with us?"

"God revealed to Mrs. White some interesting things about those last days on earth," said Mother. "Maybe they will answer your question.

"God showed her that just before Jesus comes, thick blackness will blanket the entire earth. People will be afraid and stumble around in the darkness. Then a rainbow will slice through the heavens. It will encircle each little praying group. God's people will hear His voice saying 'Look up!' They will see the rainbow, and they will see Jesus. Their time of deliverance has come! This will be a thrilling time for them and a terrifying time for everyone else.

"Everything in nature will be turned upside down. Nothing will be right. Streams will flow backwards. Dark clouds will clash together against each other. God's voice will say, 'It is done.' His voice shakes the entire earth. It is the most enormous earthquake ever experienced. The sky itself seems to snap open and closed. The mountains shake. Rocks are scattered everywhere. There is a huge roar. The sea whips up in fury. A hurricane shrieks. The earth heaves and swells, its crust is breaking up. Mountain chains start sinking. Inhabited islands disappear. Seaports sink under the water. At the same time, prison walls fall down, and God's people, who have been held captive, are set free."

"That sounds awesome!" said Michael. "No wonder people who don't understand what is happening are terrified."

"Suddenly they start understanding what is happening," said Mother, "and they realize too late that all this time they have been fighting against God. The graves open, and certain people are raised to life. All God's people, who have died since 1844, are resurrected to see Him return in glory. So are those who crucified Him and some of His greatest enemies through the ages. They are raised to life to see Jesus come just as He said He would. This second group will look the same as they did when they died.

"On the other hand, although God's people will be resurrected the same height as they were when they died, they will have all the freshness and energy of a young person, without any blemishes or deformities."

"So Grandma Jo will still be short," said Michael, "but she'll have hair again."

"Right," said Mother, smiling. "Jesus is going to take his people home with Him. They will get to eat from the tree of life and grow up into the humans they could have been if they had not lived on such a sinful, polluted earth."

"Grandma Jo will get tall!" Michael said.

"And so will you," said Mother.

"All right!" said Michael. "I've always hated being short."

"Through the dark, black clouds a brilliant star appears," Mother continued. "A marvelous change comes over God's people who have been waiting for Jesus to come. A short time ago their faces were pale and anxious. Now they are glowing with wonder and love. The clouds sweep back, and everyone—righteous and wicked—sees a hand holding tables of stone. They are open so all can read God's commandments. Those who have been disobeying God's law and paying no attention to it are terrified.

"Then God's voice speaks and pronounces a blessing on His Sabbath keepers. There's a shout of victory. Next a small, black cloud appears—about half the size of a man's hand. God's people know this is the sign that Jesus is coming. They watch as the cloud comes nearer and nearer and grows brighter and more glorious. The sky becomes brilliant with thousands and thousands of angels. Soon everyone can see Jesus Himself in the cloud, shining brighter than the sun at noon. The wicked are beside themselves with fear, and even God's faithful people look around them and start to shake. 'Who can stand?' they ask."

"Do they mean who can stand up because of the earthquake and all the commotion going on in the earth?" Michael asked.

"I think they mean who is good enough to stand before such a powerful God," said Mother. "Because Jesus' voice answers them and says, 'My grace is sufficient for you.' Then the angels begin singing, and joy fills the hearts of God's people.

"The wicked people try to hide from Jesus; they begin shouting for the rocks and mountains to fall on them and cover them up. Those who once laughed at Jesus when He hung on the cross are silent now. Priests and rulers remember the part they played in His crucifixion, and in terror they try to hide.

"Then Jesus calls out to all His faithful people who have been sleeping through the years in death. 'Awake! Awake!' He shouts. 'Get up, you who are sleeping in the ground!' And they do arise—all the righteous people who have ever lived are raised to life, from Adam right down to the present. They will never die again. Little children who have died will be carried by the angels and placed in their mother's arms.

"Also, the good people, who are alive on the earth when Jesus comes and who never died, will be changed in less time than it takes to blink your eye. God will give us immortality; we will never die."

"Wow!" said Michael. "I can hardly wait."

"Me too," agreed Mother. "Friends and loved ones who have been separated by death will be together again. The people who have died loving God and believing in Him will rise into the air first. Then we who are alive will be caught up with them and will all move toward heaven together."

"Will we just float through the air," asked Michael, "or do we go to heaven in a space ship or something?"

"I don't know," said Mother. "Mrs. White talks about us going to heaven in a chariot that sings 'holy, holy, holy' as it goes upward toward heaven. She calls it a 'cloudy chariot.' I'm not sure what that means, but she says the chariot sings as it moves along and that angels will go with it and sing too. Of course, neither John in Revelation nor Mrs. White in the 1800s would have known how to describe a spaceship. So a 'chariot' could mean a lot of things. But whatever it is, we know that it will be a lot more sophisticated than anything humans have ever built."

"Sure," said Michael, "because God is smarter than any humans ever have been."

"Mrs. White tells us that before entering the city of God, we will all gather and stand in a huge square with Jesus in the middle."

"I bet we'll all be able to see Him from where we're standing," said Michael.

"Definitely," said Mother. "And Jesus will hand us emblems of our victory."

Jesus Is Coming!

"What are 'emblems of victory'?" asked Michael.

"Well," said Mother. "Here on earth sometimes we give statues or awards or cups to people who have achieved something outstanding."

"Oh, I get it," said Michael. "Like blue ribbons and stuff. It means that we're winners."

"Yes," said Mother, "something like that. I don't know just what these emblems of victory will be. Jesus will also give us a royal insignia because we are royalty, sons and daughters of the King of the universe. And He will give us crowns. We are also told that He will give us a new name."

"That's great for people who never liked their name," said Michael.

"I think," said Mother, "that we will each have a special name that will be a secret between Jesus and us. Because He knows us better than anyone else, He will be able to give us a name that really fits our personality and the experiences we have had with Him. Our crowns will say 'Holiness to the Lord' on them. Jesus will also give us a palm branch and a harp."

Michael started laughing.

"What's so funny?" asked Mother.

"Well, since I play the trombone, I sometimes tease people who play stringed instruments. I've always said wind instruments were the coolest. But it sounds like when I go to heaven, I'm going to be playing a stringed instrument after all."

Mother laughed too. "Yes," she said, "but it will be the neatest stringed instrument you have ever seen!

"Then Jesus will open the gate and welcome us to the city. He will be welcoming Adam too. Mrs. White tells us that He's going to take Adam back to his Garden of Eden. Jesus has saved the very garden that He created for Adam in the first place. Adam will walk around the garden and recognize the very same trees that he took care of way back in the beginning before everything was ruined by sin. Jesus will lead Adam over to the tree of life and feed him from it. Adam had to leave Eden because God didn't want him to eat from the tree of life and make sin last forever. But now that sin has gone, he can eat from it and live forever with Jesus."

"Wow!" said Michael. "It's like everything is put back the way it was before sin happened."

"That's right," said Mom. "Adam will be so excited. He will throw his crown at Jesus' feet and hug Him. Then we'll all sing praises to Jesus. And we humans from earth will sing the song of deliverance. The Bible calls it the song of Moses and the Lamb. The angels will have to stop singing then because no one else can really understand what we know. No one else has been forgiven and loved as much as we have been."

"I can almost see the city," said Michael, "and hear the music. Just think, we'll get to see Jesus!"

41

One Thousand Years

"Is the story all over after we get to heaven and God's city?" asked Michael.

"Oh no," said Mother. "What about Satan?"

"Oh yeah," said Michael. "All of God's people who have died, plus all of His people who are still alive, will rise into the air with Jesus. What will happen to everyone who is left on the earth?"

"They will be filled with tremendous regret—not because they love God, but because they are going to miss eternal life. They realize they have been deceived and start blaming one another—especially the pastors and church leaders who had misled them. Soon the wicked people die from the brightness of Jesus' coming. Remember the story of the scapegoat who was sent out in the wilderness?"

"Yes," said Michael. "For atonement they took two goats, God's goat and the scapegoat. God's goat was sacrificed, and its blood was taken into the Most Holy Place. But not the scapegoat. All the forgiven sins of the people were transferred onto that goat, and he was sent out into the wilderness to wander around alone."

"That's right," said Mother. "This is the time in history when that prophecy is fulfilled."

"That was a picture prophecy," said Michael.

"Yes," said Mother. "God likes to use those. So the sins of God's people will be placed on Satan, and he will be banished to the earth, which will be like a wilderness after all the earthquakes and destruction happening just before Jesus comes. Satan will be alone with his angry angels, who will blame him for everything that has happened. The Bible talks about this in Revelation 20:1-3."

Michael read, "I saw an angel coming down from heaven. He had the key to the bottomless pit. He also held a large chain in his hand. The angel grabbed the dragon, that old snake who is the devil. The angel tied him up for 1,000 years. Then he threw him into the bottomless pit and closed it and locked it over him. The angel did this so that he could not trick the people of the earth anymore until the 1,000 years were ended. After 1,000 years he must be set free for a short time."

"John describes the earth at this time as a 'bottomless pit.' So Satan and his angels will be alone on the destroyed earth for a thousand years," said Mother.

"That's a long time," said Michael. "That's longer than any jail sentence a human could have. What will we be doing during that time?"

"We will be in heaven with Jesus," said Mother. "During the 1,000 years God will answer all our questions."

"So we'll get to look through the heavenly videotapes and understand what really happened?" asked Michael.

"Yes," said Mother. "Revelation 20:4, 6 describes this."

Michael turned to the verses in Revelation and read, "Then I saw some thrones and people sitting on them. They had been given the power to judge. And I saw the souls of those who had been killed because they were faithful to the truth of Jesus and the message from God. They had not worshiped the beast or his idol. They had not received the mark of the beast on their foreheads or in their hands. They came back to life and ruled with Christ for 1,000 years. . . . Blessed and holy are those who share in this first raising of the dead. The second death has no power over them. They will be priests for God and for Christ. They will rule with Him for 1,000 years."

"Good," said Mother. "Now read 1 Corinthians 6:2, 3."

"Surely you know that God's people will judge the world." "When the Bible talks about us judging men and angels, it means the bad angels and the bad people who have died on the earth, doesn't it?" asked Michael.

"Yes," said Mother. "We will look through all the decisions God made and see how fair He was. And during this time God is going to help us understand everything that has happened."

"I'm glad," said Michael. "There are lots of things I don't understand. I'm sure other people have questions to ask Him too. Meanwhile, I guess I just need to count on the fact that He loves me and that He is fair and that someday He'll explain everything to me."

42

The War
Is Over!

"This is the last chapter of the story, isn't it?" exclaimed Michael.

Mother nodded. "At the end of the thousand years, we will have had the opportunity to ask all the questions we want. We'll understand why things have happened as they have. But God still needs to finish things up. Satan is still 'in jail' on the destroyed earth, and the people who chose not to follow God's way are lying dead on the earth. The rest of us have become grown-up saints by this time."

"Wow," said Michael, "imagine how we'll grow and become healthy in a perfect place like that. And we'll eat from the tree of life!"

"Yes," said Mother. "Now it is time for Jesus' third advent."

"A third advent?" asked Michael.

"Yes," said Mother. "His first advent was when He came as a baby to Bethlehem. The second advent will be when He comes to take us to heaven with Him. And the third advent will be when He comes back to earth with us and the New Jerusalem for the final judgment that will permanently end the controversy. Zechariah 14:4, 9 describe what happens when Jesus comes back to earth the third time."

"I'll read it," said Michael. "On that day he will stand on the Mount of Olives, east of Jerusalem. The Mount of Olives will split in two. A deep valley will run east and west. Half the mountain will move north. And half will move south. . . .

"Then the Lord will be king over the whole world. At that time there will be only one Lord. And his name will be the only name."

"You see," said Mother, "this time Jesus won't just come in the clouds. He will actually touch down on the Mount of Olives in Israel and split it wide open to form a plain. All the people who chose not to follow Him and who were destroyed when He came the second time will now come back to life. They will have the same diseases and look the same as they did when they died."

"If they had a second chance now," asked Michael, "do you think they would choose any differently?"

"No," said Mother. "God gave everyone enough time to make up their minds for sure. They would make the same choices even if they were given another chance."

"Imagine how they'll look," interrupted Michael. "There'll be giants from before Noah's flood, and all of the really bad people like Hitler and Genghis Khan will be there too."

"And they will be just as rebellious when they come back to life as they were before," said Mother. "Satan will lead them to plan an attack. Skillful workers will make weapons. Military leaders will organize everyone into companies and divisions. It will be the largest army in earth's history."

"What will they plan to attack?" Michael wanted to know.

"They will plan to attack the New Jerusalem with Jesus in it," said Mother. "The battle isn't over yet. They will still be fighting God."

"You'd think they would realize by now that they can't win," Michael said.

"Apparently not," said Mother. "Jesus will command that the

gates to the New Jerusalem be closed. Satan's forces will surround the city for the final battle. 'We can take it!' they shout. And they will begin their attack with military precision."

"Will we be scared?" asked Michael.

"Oh no," said Mother. "We have already learned that God can take care of us no matter what. Inside the city we will be singing. All of us know that we are not there because of anything we did, or our own goodness. We will be there by God's goodness and the mercy He showed in sending His Son to die in place of us.

"Then high above the walls where everyone inside and outside can see, Jesus will be crowned the King of kings with supreme majesty and power. Then He will pronounce the sentence against those who rebelled against His government and oppressed His people. The Bible says the books of heaven will be opened. The people surrounding the city will be conscious of every sin they ever committed. Above God's throne will appear something like a giant video screen. Everyone will see his own life. The heavenly movie archives will show the whole story from Adam's fall to Jesus' perfect life and the people who tortured Him to death. The movie will continue right down to the last day of earth's history. The wicked people will be horrified, but they won't be able to turn away. They will have to continue watching themselves and all the terrible things they have done."

"Awful!" said Michael. "King Herod will have to watch all those babies being killed."

"And another King Herod will have to see himself cause John the Baptist's death," said Mother.

"And Pilate will have to watch himself reject Jesus all over again. And the soldiers who killed Him and the Jews who were shouting and teasing Him," added Michael.

"But remember," said Mother, "some of them repented afterwards and became Jesus' followers. Emperor Nero will be there. He will see all of those he tortured and killed who are now singing inside the Holy City. As all of these memories play on the heavenly video screens, sinners will realize that Satan has been a failure. The whole conflict from the beginning has been about Satan's need to justify himself. He tried to prove that God's government was responsible for his rebellion and that God was to blame for all of the sadness and suffering in the world. But as everyone watches the records, they will realize how wrong he was. They will see what they have missed by being slaves to Satan instead of choosing to be the children of God.

"Jesus will look around at His people inside the city, all of them renewed in His image. In a voice loud enough for everyone inside and outside to hear, Jesus will say, 'Look at the ones I bought with My own blood. I died so that they could live with me forever.' Then all of us will sing a song of praise to Jesus."

"What happens next?" asked Michael.

"Every person outside the walls, from the simplest to the greatest, will bow down and acknowledge that God is just and that Satan is wrong. Even Satan will admit that.

"But then," continued Mother, "Satan will make one last effort to capture the city. He will urge all the wicked people to fight. But now they are all angry with him. Let's read what the Bible tells us in Ezekiel 28:6-8 and 16-19."

Michael read, "So this is what the Lord God says: You think you are wise like a god. But I will bring foreign people against you. They will be the cruelest nation. They will pull out their swords and destroy all that your wisdom has built. And they will dishonor your greatness. They will kill you. You will die a terrible death like those who are killed at sea. . . .

"Because you traded with countries far away, you learned to be cruel, and you sinned. So I threw you down in disgrace from the mountain of God. And the living creature who guarded you forced you out from among the gems of fire. You became too proud because of your beauty. You ruined your wisdom because of your greatness. I threw you down to the ground. Your example taught a lesson to other kings. You dishonored your places of worship through your many sins and dishonest trade. So I set your city on fire. And it burned up. I turned you into ashes on the ground for all those watching to see. All the nations who knew you are shocked about you. Your punishment was so terrible. And you are gone forever." "Is this talking about Satan?" asked Michael.

"Yes," said Mother, "And remember that all the confessed and forgiven sins of God's people have been transferred onto Satan, just as was pictured by the scapegoat in the wilderness. Satan will be punished not only for his sins but for the sins of God's forgiven people whom he deceived.

"Fire will come down from heaven and burn up everything that is left of sin. This sounds terrible, but really Jesus is doing the most merciful thing He can. These people would be miserable in God's new world. They would hate living where everyone is pure and happy. And they would just cause more trouble.

Because of his terrible sins and all the suffering he caused on the earth, Satan will be the last one to die. But sin and sinners will finally be gone. The only reminder we will have of sin and the terrible things that have happened will be the scars on Jesus' hands and feet and side. Those will be there forever."

"Is that the end?" asked Michael.

"Not yet," said Mother. "Then Jesus will recreate our earth."

"Like He did in Genesis?" asked Michael.

"Maybe," said Mother. "Except this time we will be able to watch Him. Several Bible verses tell us what life will be like in this new world. Revelation 21:4 says, 'He will wipe away every tear from their eyes. There will be no more death, sadness, crying, or pain. All the old ways are gone.' Now you read Isaiah 62:3."

Michael read, "You will be like a beautiful crown in the Lord's hand. You will be like a king's crown in your God's hand."

Then Mother read Isaiah 65:19. "I will rejoice over Jerusalem. I will be delighted with my people. There will never again be crying and sadness in that city." "Now, Michael, you read what Revelation 21:11, 24 says about God's city, the new Jerusalem."

The War Is Over!

"It was shining with the glory of God. It was shining bright like a very expensive jewel, like a jasper. It was clear as crystal. . . . By its light the people of the world will walk. The kings of the earth will bring their glory into it."

"Mrs. White says that we will be able to fly and visit other worlds," said Mother.

"Really fly?" asked Michael. "That will be so cool! What else will we do?"

"We'll be able to build houses. Imagine being able to design and build just the kind of place you'd like to live in—and being able to live there forever! We'll plant gardens and eat the things we grow. We'll never get tired or sick or discouraged or sad. We'll have all the energy to do anything we want to—and all the time we need to carry out any project we start. We'll get to travel, even to other worlds, and we can tell them about how Jesus saved us and how wonderful He is. Salvation will be something we will have experienced that no one else in the universe will be able to understand as we do. We'll be able to study nature and learn all kinds of new things.

"Actually," said Mother, "we can't begin to imagine how amazing life on the new earth is going to be. It will be far better than our best thoughts about it. In God's new world, everything will grow and get better—knowledge, love, reverence, and happiness. And the more we get to know God, the more we will love Him. We will be happier and happier and happier.

"Now the controversy will finally be over. The battle will be finished. The war will be won. Everything will finally be settled, and it will be proved once and for all that God is love."

"That's the best story in the world. I'm so glad it is true," said Michael. "It answers all my questions."

"I'm sure you will think of more questions," said Mother, "and many of them I won't be able to answer."

"But Jesus will, someday," said Michael. "And I am going to be there to ask them."

If you enjoyed this book,
you'll also enjoy these other books:

Ellen: the Girl With Two Angels
ISBN 0-8163-1325-3
$5.99US/$8.99Cdn

Detective Zack Series
$6.99US/$$10.49Cdn
The Secret of Noah's Flood
The Secret in the Sand
The Red Hat Mystery
The Mystery at Thunder Mountain
The Missing Manger Mystery
Danger at Dinosaur Camp
The Secret in the Storm
The Mystery on the Midway
Trapped in Darkmoor Manor
Secret of Blackloch Castle

Order from your ABC by calling **1-800-765-6955**, or get on-line
and shop our virtual store at **www.adventistbookcenter.com**.
  • Read a chapter from your favorite book
  • Order on-line
  • Sign up for email notices on new products